TEST SKILLS

THE
WORLD
BOOK

Learning Library

Volume
4
TEST SKILLS

Published by
World Book, Inc.
a Scott Fetzer company
Chicago

Staff

Publisher
William H. Nault

Editorial

Editor in Chief
Robert O. Zeleny

Executive Editor
Dominic J. Miccolis

Associate Editor
Maureen M. Mostyn

Senior Editor
Michael K. Urban

Contributing Editor
Sevasti Spanos

Production Editor
Elizabeth Ireland

Index Editor
Joyce Goldenstern

Permissions Editor
Janet T. Peterson

Editorial Assistant
Elizabeth Lepkowski

Art

Executive Art Director
William Hammond

Designers
Tessing Design, Inc.

Production Artist
Cynthia Schultz

Photography Director
John S. Marshall

Photographer
Don Sala

Product Production

Executive Director
Peter Mollman

Manufacturing
Joseph C. La Count, director

Research and Development
Henry Koval, manager

Pre-Press Services
Jerry Stack, director
Randi Park
Sandra Van den Broucke

Proofreaders
Marguerite Hoye, head
Ann Dillon
Esther Johns
Daniel Marotta

Copyright © 1986 by
World Book, Inc.
Merchandise Mart Plaza
Chicago, Illinois 60654

Printed in the United States of America

ISBN 0-7166-3188-1 (Volume 4)
ISBN 0-7166-3184-9 (set)
Library of Congress Catalog No. 86-50558
d/hh

Contents

Introduction	7
Section I Successful Testing	8
Section II Test-Taking Tips	16
Section III Teachers' Tests	34
Section IV Standardized Tests	76
Test Terms	119
Index	124

Acknowledgments

The answer sheet that appears in photographs on pages 33 and 76–77 is from *Primary Mental Abilities,* answer sheet for Grades 6–9, by Thelma Gwinn Thurstone. © 1962 by Thelma Gwinn Thurstone. Reprinted by permission of the publisher, Science Research Associates, Inc.

Introduction

Your success in school is often measured by the tests you take. Teachers and other educators evaluate your progress and capabilities by examining your test results. It is extremely important that you perform well on tests throughout your years in school. This volume can help you improve your basic skills in test taking.

The first section, "Successful Testing," puts you in the correct frame of mind for testing, and it explains the difference between teachers' and standardized tests. The second section is entitled "Test-Taking Tips," and it gives useful pointers on general preparation for tests and actual techniques to use while you are taking an examination.

Teachers' tests is the subject of the third section. You will learn about the many different types of tests that your teacher gives you, and you will receive useful information on how to tackle different types of test items, such as multiple-choice, short-answer, and essay items.

The final section gives you a clear picture of what to expect when you take standardized tests. Thirteen common standardized test items, like verbal analogy items and number series items, are presented. Strategies for doing well on each type of item are given along with examples or descriptions of the items themselves.

Start now to try to improve your performance on tests. This volume should point you in the right direction and give you the information and background you need to become a top-knotch test taker.

I SUCCESSFUL TESTING

This section provides an overview of testing, and it explains the difference between teachers' and standardized tests.

Your Viewpoint in Testing   **11**
Teachers' and Standardized Tests   **13**
Terms in Testing   **15**

Successful Testing

ave you ever tried to count all the different kinds of tests you take each year? There are many. First, think of the tests your teachers give you. There are so many kinds, in so many different subjects, that you may be unable to count them all. But do you know what you can do? Test well, no matter who you are or what your test is about.

Besides teachers' tests, what other kinds of tests do you take? Most students take standardized tests. These tests are often purchased by schools and given to a great number of students. Designed to give consistent results, they are easy to use and quick to score. They are much a part of today's school testing.

The people who make standardized tests are not teachers at your school. You do not know them and probably never will. These test makers are scientists, and their job is a big one. The standardized tests they make cover much more territory than teachers' tests do, and the tests have many more purposes. Standardized tests, for example, may be designed to measure what you know, how easily you can learn—or even what you are like.

Do you worry about how you can do well on a standardized test, when it is made by someone you have never seen, someone who has never taught you anything? Don't worry. You can perform well. Top-notch testing is always possible for you, and this publication is going to show you why that is so.

You are about to learn the basic ingredients everyone needs to test well on both teachers' tests and standardized tests. You will discover something you may never have known before: You can be calm, comfortable, and confident—whenever you take a test.

Your Viewpoint in Testing

Of much importance to you is understanding that good test performance does not necessarily mean gaining the highest scores in your group. Good performance means scores that are at the highest level you can and should reach according to your ability and goals.

Be Interested

Good performance is a personal matter. To test well, you have to become concerned about your testing progress. If you are concerned, you will be motivated to do the best you can.

Remember, tests are designed for you. As the test taker, you are the focus of all the work that goes into your tests. The test makers, whether they are at school or elsewhere, are essential parts of the process, but you are the most important person involved in your tests.

Be Positive

Do you ever feel that tests keep you from doing what you want to do? Do they prevent you, for example, from getting good grades, qualifying for sports, or being able to go to the movies on a weeknight? You have to reverse this way of thinking if you are going to be successful on tests. Tests are designed to work for you, not against you.

Tests identify your strengths and weaknesses. They show if you can handle your course work and additional activities. They help you adjust to meeting your responsibilities so you can enjoy your leisure. Be positive about tests. They will help you as much as you let them.

Tests are designed to work for you, not against you.

Be Realistic

Each person is unique. Your abilities and interests differ from those of any other person. Set your testing expectations according to what your abilities and interests are. Be realistic about your performance level on any test.

Your expectations for a test score are based on what you believe, after careful thought and preparation, is possible for you. If your scores on vocabulary tests have always been low and you have done nothing to improve your knowledge and skill with words, it is unrealistic to believe that your score in vocabulary will improve on this week's test. If you have studied hard to improve your knowledge and skills, expecting a better score on vocabulary on your next test is realistic. After a good deal of study that takes place over a number of months, your scores may greatly improve, but this process takes time. Just as the pole-vaulter raises the level of the jump after one height has been achieved, so you can set your expectations higher and higher as your scores gradually become better.

Set Your Goals

Perhaps you already have excellent abilities in mathematics computation. Practice through testing may provide you with more speed and accuracy when doing this type of problem. Your success has enabled you to set your sights on a future goal. You want to work in a career involving mathematics.

You try to score as high as you can in this subject. You need to learn as much of the material as well as you can. Knowing it is essential to the work you someday wish to do. Your score shows you are succeeding.

In the future, schools may look at the scores you received in mathematics tests to determine whether you can do the work necessary to achieve your educational and career goals. Whether you are admitted to a school may depend in the long run on your mathematics scores.

At the same time, your best friend is showing every sign of being a gifted gymnast. She practices day and night. Her mathematics understanding and skills are acceptable, but not exceptional. Should she take time from her practice in order to study so that her mathematics scores can become as high as yours?

As you learned before, testing is a personal matter. Your friend should make her decisions based not on whether she scores so highly as you on tests but on what her goals are. Excellence in mathematics may be among them, of course. She may be good in mathematics and gymnastics. But if not, medium scores in mathematics may be enough for her. Your success should not be a factor in her decisions, any more than her success in athletics should figure in yours. If you are not very coordinated, medium scores in physical education drills are realistic and appropriate for you.

Teachers' and Standardized Tests

So far you have learned about how you fit into the testing picture. You know yours is the most important role, though there are other people who participate in testing. You know four good ways of looking at tests: with interest, with resolve, with practicality, and with an eye to the future.

Now you are going to learn in depth about the two basic groups into which you can place almost all the tests you take in school: teachers' tests and standardized tests. The first is perhaps easier for you to understand.

Teachers' Tests

Most of the tests you take in school are teacher-made or teacher-selected tests. Teacher-made tests range from pop quizzes the teacher makes up and writes on the chalkboard to typewritten examinations prepared to test your knowledge of an entire term's work.

Teacher-made tests can also be oral. The teacher, for example, may ask you questions in a foreign language and require oral responses from you that will be graded.

The teacher is often the only one who decides what to put in a teacher-made test. But teachers do not make teacher-selected tests. They choose them. Teacher-selected tests are sometimes taken on computer. They may be part of a computer-learning program at your school. Teachers also give tests that come with classroom texts. These tests may be presented in special test booklets that are passed out to students on testing days.

Teacher-selected tests have been developed by educational writers and carefully chosen by your teacher because they appear to offer valid ways of determining your progress in the class. For these tests, the educational writers at the publishing companies are the test makers, and the teacher is the test user. You are, of course, the test taker.

A standardized test is designed to provide a standard, or uniform, measure of performance.

Teacher-made and teacher-selected tests are both designed to measure how much each student is learning in the classroom. This is one reason these tests are sometimes called classroom tests.

Standardized Tests

Teachers, counselors, and other educators need to make decisions about your school progress. Some involve comparisons. The educators, for example, may need to see how the students in your school district are doing in comparison with students in another school district. Educators may also want to see how well the students in their school district have learned a specific body of information or whether they have developed specific skills.

To measure this type of progress, educators must make sure all students in their school district take the test according to the same standards, or agreed-upon rules. A standardized test is designed to provide a standard, or uniform, measure of performance. Every student should take the test according to the same directions, the same rules, and the same testing conditions.

Scientists called psychometrists develop standardized tests. Educators select and give them. There are several kinds of standardized tests from which to choose.

Some teacher-selected tests given as part of course work are standardized. But you are probably most familiar with standardized tests given to many classes in your school district. The most common are standardized tests of achievement. These are designed to measure how much a large number of students have already learned about a school subject. Many of your teachers' tests, standardized or nonstandardized, are also achievement tests.

Another widely known standardized test is designed to measure your ability to learn school subjects. These tests try to predict your future success in school by measuring your ability, or aptitude, to do well in specific learning areas. These tests, which may also measure your interests, are called standardized tests of aptitude (and interest).

Other standardized tests include those that measure your general learning ability (sometimes measured as your intelligence quotient, or IQ), your ability to progress to a higher level of learning (your competency), and your personality.

Do not be misled by personality or IQ tests in magazines or newspapers. They are not standardized and do not have the accuracy of the standardized tests that are described in this book.

Terms in Testing

As you begin to learn more about testing, you will be introduced to many terms that may be new to you. Like any area of study, testing has its own vocabulary. Some test terms you meet may appear new and difficult. Others will be words that you know but that seem to be used in a way slightly different from what you are used to.

Look up any unfamiliar test terms at the end of this book.

Should you come across any unfamiliar terms in these pages, look them up in "Test Terms" at the end of this book. Soon they will be part of your working vocabulary.

Let there be no doubt about it. Understanding testing is a challenge, but one that you can meet with effort and the help of this useful book. Are you ready to start? Then get comfortable. It is time to talk about test-taking tips.

II TEST-TAKING TIPS

Tips to becoming a better test taker are the subject of this section. Topics include general preparation for tests and techniques to use during actual examinations.

Taking Teachers' Tests 18

Taking Standardized Tests 30

Test-Taking Tips

*G*ood *test takers have good test-taking skills. These students generally are able to relax and think logically, study efficiently, and read their tests accurately. Good test takers are also usually up to the physical demands testing places on them.*

Let's look at how you can become a better test taker. Many of the guidelines presented here for teachers' tests also apply to standardized tests. Some special tips about taking standardized tests will end this section.

Taking Teachers' Tests

Test Content

There are many ways to find out what might be covered on a test. First, ask questions. Get whatever information you can from your teachers. They may show you previous tests as a kind of review or, if asked, tell you the exact kinds of questions that will be on a test.

During review sessions, your teachers are likely to emphasize what they consider important. They will give clues such as "Write this down," or "You will want to remember," or "You will have to know."

Sometimes your teachers will spend much time using visual aids to make specific points or emphasize particular ideas. Write these aids down in your class notes. The notes, previous quizzes on the same material, and the topics discussed in class can help you come up with a list of areas that have been given importance. On the test, you can probably expect to find questions covering these areas. And you will have developed a sixth sense about the kinds of questions your teachers will ask.

Study Planning

When you have a good idea of what to study, think about organizing your review time. You want to have enough review time to be able to go over all of the available material before the test.

Study Schedule

Decide when in the day you feel most alert. Schedule at least part of your studying at that time. If you are a morning person, perhaps you can do some work before school. If you do better later in the day, then plan to study after school or at night before you go to bed.

Once you plan your study time, stick to your plan.

If you have household responsibilities or after-school activities, ask your teachers, counselors, and parents to help you with your study schedule so you can get everything in. Once you plan your study time, stick to your plan.

Study Place

If you do not already have a regular study place, now is the time to set one up. Perhaps you can share a space with your brother or sister, or maybe you can use the same area in shifts.

Basically, you need a place with good light where you will be comfortable. You need a work space and a place to keep your materials. Naturally, it is best to have as much quiet as possible. If you cannot avoid household distractions, you may have to study somewhere else.

When you have a place to study, gather all the materials you will need and take them there. Keep them there, if possible. Having everything you need before you start will avoid interruptions like searching for a ruler or eraser.

Reference File

Keep your classwork papers, tests, quizzes, reports, notes, and corrected homework in a drawer, folder, or box in your study location. When it is time to begin serious study for a test, your reference file will be there, full of important information.

Learning Techniques

Homework

Homework is a cornerstone of much learning. The assignments are relatively short, but they cover the basics of what you are learning at school. Your homework assignments are key indicators of what will be on your tests. If you master your homework, you will master your tests.

Homework assignments are key indicators of what will be on your tests.

Keep a small notebook to record what your daily assignments are. Do them to your best ability. Correct them the next day in class. Organize your homework in a large notebook and store it in your reference file.

Notes

Notes are your record of the important issues or ideas that have been emphasized in class discussions and other activities. But in order for your notes to be meaningful, they must be well organized. The more you take and organize notes, the better you will become at it.

Outlines

Another important technique is outlining. A good outline is especially useful for studying because it organizes much material in a rather small space. Here is some help in making a study outline.

The outline should contain all the material to be covered on the test. Draw a line down the center of a piece of paper. On the left side, write down the most important topics. On the right, write as many details as you can that will serve as clues to remind you of information you are learning. A good study outline should include relatively few main topics and a way of showing how one part of the information relates to another.

After writing your outline, cover up the left side of the paper. Read the details on the right side. On another sheet of paper, try to write down the headings that fit the details. Then, cover the right side of the paper and write a summary of the information that belongs with each heading you have written.

Memorizing

Memorizing is an important skill. Whether you have to learn a poem or information for a test, these hints can help you memorize:

1. Know that you can do it—be positive.
2. Understand the subject.
3. Have a plan of attack.
4. Organize materials.
5. Concentrate fully.
6. Work—do not waste time worrying.
7. Use the senses to memorize. Read to yourself. Read aloud. Listen to tapes.
8. Pace yourself.
9. Practice—practice—practice.

Daily Review

A good way to give your memory a boost is daily review. A good daily review helps you remember the highlights from class lessons. And you have a better chance to correct errors and fill gaps in your skills and knowledge. If you find that you have problems in a specific area, you have time to seek help and advice from your teachers. With your school counselor, you can work out any test-taking problems you might have.

Flashcards

Another good way to memorize is to make flashcards from index cards. Write questions on the front and answers on the back. Try to make up questions that will serve as a good review when test time nears.

Flashcards are good for learning vocabulary, lists, dates, names, mathematics rules, grammar rules, brief literature summaries, science information, and historical facts. For each subject, prepare a separate pile of cards. Keep them in your reference file.

Study Aid

School Counselors

School counselors are trained to understand tests and students' study problems. A counselor can help students identify study weaknesses and give advice about what to expect on tests. Counselors can also help students overcome anxiety. Many books, guides, and pamphlets line the guidance counselor's bookshelves. Use them as resources.

Study Groups

Sometimes it is helpful if you and your friends form a study group. You can meet before tests or throughout the year as part of a study routine. There are problems to be avoided, however. For a group study session to benefit everyone, these guidelines are necessary:

Use your textbook to give yourself practice tests.

1. A study group will work better when no more than five students take part. A smaller group gives more opportunity for everyone to take an active role.

2. Each group should consist of students who are close in ability and motivation. This lessens the chance that one or two strong personalities will take over.

3. The group should agree to stick to its topics. Each should be discussed separately and in order. No socializing should go on during a group study session.

4. There should be an agreed-upon plan. Each member can bring a study outline, for example. From the outlines, a more detailed outline can be created for everyone. For discussion, all members can bring questions or problems that have been giving them trouble. If there are disagreements or weak areas in knowledge, they can be researched before the next session.

Textbooks

Many of your school subjects will be taught with the aid of a textbook. Chances are, if you are assigned a textbook of some kind, it will be useful for studying for tests.

Reading assigned pages is important. But there are many ways that you can use your textbook. One is to note the paragraph headings, which help you outline the material you are studying. Other aids in outlining are the chapter titles; end-of-chapter summaries; end-of-chapter questions; glossaries; material printed in **boldface** type or in *italics;* and illustrations such as maps, graphs, charts, and diagrams, plus the captions to those illustrations.

You can use your textbook to give yourself practice tests. Rewrite questions and problems that appear in your book and test yourself. When you run into difficulties, go back over the material that deals with the problem area.

Tutors

Friends and family can tutor you. But, if you are considering hiring a tutor, it is often best to get some suggestions from school. Teachers, counselors, or others in the school office may have a list of qualified tutors. You may be able to find out payment rates and available time slots from these sources, also.

If you and your parents have limited money for a tutor, be sure to say so. Sometimes schools can arrange for older, qualified students to tutor for a small fee or extra credit in one of their classes. Counselors also often know of community organizations that offer tutoring at little or no cost.

When you meet your tutor, be frank. Explain what your exact problem is. If you have any papers that show the problem, share them. Find out whether the tutor feels confident that you can improve in the time available. Then set up your schedule carefully. Make sure that you both agree on hours, fee, and place.

Other Study Hints

1. Go over the papers in your reference file and make sure you understand why you were marked off on any paper. Go over all your notes and homework.

2. Keep your flashcards until the end of the term and use them to study for final exams. Revise or add to them as necessary.

3. If you own or can borrow a tape recorder, use it to make a question tape. Record questions from your book, from old tests and quizzes, from your flashcards, and from notes. After each question, leave some empty tape space for answering time, depending on the length of the answer. When you have recorded all your questions, play the tape back and try to answer the questions orally or in writing. If you want no time limit on your answers, omit the answer time on the tape as you record. Then just push the stop button after each question when you replay the tape. When you have answered the question to your satisfaction, play the next question.

4. Some other materials that may be available for your use are: computer learning programs; teaching machines; learning tapes for foreign language, reading, music, and other subjects; videos, filmstrips, films, or slide programs; learning games that your teacher may keep in your classroom; and old workbooks that the teacher or school librarian might make available for your use.

5. Use whatever human resources are available to you. Be sure to ask your teacher, counselor, or family members for help if you are in trouble with a subject. If you have begun your study sessions early enough, you will have time to find the help you need.

Cramming

Cramming defeats the purpose of education. Your mind cannot be forced to do short-cut learning. What you learn through cramming rarely sticks. In the long run, your personal goals are short-changed. You are not building a foundation on which you can build future learning.

Planned study makes cramming unnecessary. Start your review for a test as soon as possible. Do not stall with the old excuse about being too busy. Everyone is always busy doing something. But you have some reviewing to do for that test.

Health and Outlook

Your brain works best when your body is well cared for. Your body needs rest, nourishment, and healthy exercise—which you must provide. If good health habits are built into your daily life, you will most likely be mentally ready for any situation, including tests.

Allow your mind to rest before a test.

Allow your mind to rest before a test. And don't skimp on sleep. A good night's rest will make it easier for you to feel relaxed and confident.

Most students do better if they are not hungry during the test period. Don't skip meals. Don't overeat, either. A full stomach can make you sluggish.

Being emotionally prepared for a test is as important as being physically and intellectually prepared. You will do better if you are confident going in. It is a waste of energy to worry about doing poorly. Worry distracts your mind from its job: answering questions. Instead of worrying at test time, be concerned long before. Prepare properly.

Test Day

Supplies

Find out what your teacher wants you to work with. Only the most careless students come to a test without at least a sharpened pencil or a working pen. Also bring spares and an eraser. Other supplies could include a ruler, graph paper, scratch paper, or paper for writing long answers.

If you are going to need a dictionary, calculator, compass, protractor, or other aid, be sure to bring it. Although your teacher may have some extra equipment for students who forget, it is best to bring your own materials.

Test Location

Double-check the location where the test will be given if the test site is other than your classroom. Your teacher may be working with other teachers and giving the same test to more than one class.

Promptness

For most tests, it is best to arrive close to the time the test begins. Arrive with just enough time to get settled.

Understand the test directions.

Arriving early to go over your material is a bad idea. Other students may be there to socialize. Last-minute quizzing from friends can also confuse you. One of your friends may disagree with what you have learned and make you lose your self-confidence.

Arriving late for a test is always foolish. Some teachers will not permit you to take a test if you arrive late. If you are permitted, you may have to spend valuable time catching your breath and just getting organized. You will probably have missed the directions and other hints the teacher gave students who were on time.

General Instructions

The first concern when you receive the test is to listen for general instructions. Your teacher will probably tell you to write your name and may also require other information according to your grade level: date, class period, or student number.

Test Directions

Next, understand the test directions. Your teacher will probably allow you to ask questions about anything you do not understand. Even if you have a thorough knowledge of the material being tested, you can miss points if you misunderstand the tasks you are given to do.

When listening to or reading directions, it is important to be alert for key words that tell you what the teacher wants. Does the teacher want you to answer with a list of items? Or are you supposed to write an essay? If you are writing about two items, are you supposed to describe them separately or compare them? You would respond to the item "Describe the rules for playing baseball and football" differently from "Compare the rules for playing baseball and football."

If an item is unclear, your teacher may give you a sample question to demonstrate how the test should be worked. If you have no questions of your own, listen to any that your classmates ask. They might have thought of something that you missed. In any case, start working only after all the explanations have been given. You may otherwise miss something important.

Some teachers will allow students to ask questions after the test has begun, but this can cause an unfair disturbance to others. And few teachers are fooled by students who ask questions about test items in an effort to get clues for answering them.

Never ask your neighbors questions. Even if you are merely asking to borrow an eraser, you can be giving a different impression. You want no one to have the idea that you are cheating. If you need something, go to your teacher or raise your hand and ask. Cause no commotion while others work.

Scan the entire test before you begin to work.

Scanning the Test

Unless the directions of the test forbid it, scan the entire test before you begin to work. Try to find out which items are worth the most points. Spend the most time on them. The teacher may suggest the time to be spent for answering each item or section. If not, estimate it yourself, taking points into consideration.

Some items will have an indicated length, such as "in no more than half a page" or "in no more than five sentences." Stick to that length.

Remember to wear a wrist watch so that you can track your progress. You should have a written or mental timetable by which to work before you begin answering questions. Start with the easy items first to build your confidence and to make sure you don't miss any points for material you know. But make sure all your answers are in the order of the test.

Anxiety

Many students miss points because they allow anxiety to get to the point of panic. Good preparation should keep you relatively calm. But if you do find yourself frozen with fear, think positively. Pretend that you are ready to go to work. Sit up straight and hold your pen or pencil in a writing position. Read the test through once again. Answer the easy items. Starting will release your panic button. You will calm down soon and be able to handle the test.

Take your time during a test. If a question triggers your memory and ideas start flooding into your mind, jot them down on scratch paper or in the test's margins, if allowed.

Do not waste time unnecessarily, but take time to relax every 10 minutes or so, just for a few seconds. Short breaks can help your nerves and keep you alert during the test. If you have been writing a long passage, give your hand a few shakes. But don't draw attention to yourself and distract your neighbors.

Always keep your test papers neat.

Neatness

No teacher appreciates sloppy writing, so always keep your test papers neat. Misspellings, faulty punctuation, and disorganization also leave a bad impression.

Reasoning Out Answers

The first step in reasoning out an answer is to read the question carefully. If a question is long, split it into sections. If you can't answer a question, think of facts that are only indirectly related to it. They might lead to the answer.

Ask yourself some questions. What does this test item have to do with what you've learned? Does the problem illustrate an idea the class discussed in another context? Could you phrase this question in another way to make it easier to understand?

Clues

Well-written tests will hold few, if any, clues. But sometimes there are one or two. You might recognize the answer to a short-answer item in a multiple-choice item. Or a matching item might contain names or dates you can use for an essay item. Clues usually appear in multiple-choice or matching questions because of the number of choices these test items offer.

Guessing

At one time or another, you will come across a question you want to guess at. Whether to guess depends on how the test will be scored.

Most teachers base scores on the number of correct answers. If this is how your teacher is scoring, then you have nothing to lose by guessing. If the teacher has instructed you not to guess on a test, deductions are probably going to be made for wrong answers. Don't guess in this case.

When answering an essay question that you are unsure of, writing a partial answer is better than writing nothing at all. But never write nonsense. And you will be fooling no one by ending with phrases like "Time's up," as if to say if you'd had more time, you would have written more.

Running Out of Time

There are situations when you might find that you have only a few minutes left and more to do. There are ways of handling this problem.

If you are taking an objective test and there is no penalty for guessing, speed through the remaining items taking as much care as time allows. If there is a penalty, speed up, but with great care. Never make wild guesses. If you come to an item you don't know at all, skip it. Don't waste time. If you did the easy items first, your points for them are already secure.

If you are taking an essay exam, finish via a short outline for the rest of the answer and for answers you have not started. Try to get in as many ideas as possible. Abbreviate words if you have to. You may not receive full credit, but you will surely get some.

Checking Answers

Save some time to go back and check your work. It is best to wait until you have finished the entire test so that you have a break in thought. A second look later gives an answer a chance to pop out of your memory.

When checking, there are problems to avoid. Generally, your first answer on an objective test is the correct one. Consider changing it only when you are certain it is wrong. For essays, rereading is too time consuming. Trust your first thoughts and just check for spelling, punctuation, and other mechanics. If you answered the item wrong, you probably have no time to redo it now.

When the test is over and the signal has been given to stop, put down your pen or pencil. Some teachers will count off points if you work beyond the time allowed. If the test has no time limit, you may be allowed to work longer. But any test has a time limit of sorts.

Taking Standardized Tests

Helpful Sources

When you know you must take a standardized test, there are many ways to get help. As with classroom tests, teachers, counselors, study groups, tutors, and supportive family can aid you. Here are some other helpful sources.

Commercial Counseling and Tutoring Services

These services specialize in preparing students for standardized tests. They provide hints on test-taking strategies and emphasize drill in order to help students get over any test-taking anxiety they might feel. Ask your school counselor for the names of reliable commercial counseling and tutoring services.

Practice Tests

Whether from school or a test publisher, practice tests are useful in showing you the general categories of questions that will be on the test. As you read the questions, you become familiar with their organization, directions, answer sheets, and time allowances for different sections.

Marking answers properly is crucial to valid test performances. So is filling out the student identification portion of the answer sheet. Review the student identification and answer formats in your practice materials.

State Departments of Education

If you live in a state that requires competency tests, the state department of education provides information about the tests you must take. This information usually includes descriptions of the tests, grades in which tests are given, scores required to pass, and the number of times you are allowed to take the tests in order to pass. Since the state education department provides this information to local schools, you should be able to get most of the information you need from your teacher or school counselor. If you need information the local school cannot provide, then you may wish to write directly to your state department of education.

Test Publishers

Most test publishers are concerned that students understand tests and how to take them. They prepare a variety of booklets to help you. These contain instructions, sample test items, sample answer sheets, and sometimes practice tests.

Ask your teacher or counselor who publishes the test you will take. Perhaps one of them will write the company for information or give you the address so you or your parents can write.

The test publisher will not supply you with a copy of the test you will actually take. The materials that are available contain old or sample tests. Teachers and counselors also sometimes have these on hand.

University-Connected Institutes

Many universities have education departments interested in various aspects of testing for standardized or teachers' tests. These departments may sponsor clinics to help students learn test-taking skills and overcome test anxiety. Some clinics also provide learning-ability evaluation and career-counseling services. Call nearby universities about the availability of these services.

Test-Taking Books

At libraries, bookstores, and schools, you may be able to find some additional test-taking books to use with this one. But be cautious. Books on test taking sometimes outline a complicated set of rules to help you guess an answer you do not know. This approach is rarely wise. By the time you go through the process, you have wasted time you might have used to work answers that you do know. A good rule is to follow suggestions that are clear and easy. If suggestions get complicated, avoid them.

Special Problems

There are some special problems associated with taking standardized tests. You must prepare to deal with them.

Recording Answers

One mismarked answer on a standardized test's answer sheet can throw off your score for an entire section. Make sure to save enough time to check your answer sheet. This final check is not a time to rework problems and change answers. It should be brief and focused on the mechanics of filling out the sheet.

You also must erase any smudges. Since most standardized tests are machine-scored, a smudge can also throw off your score.

If you realize that part or most of your answers are mismarked due to a skipped blank or other recording error, don't panic. Fix the answer sheet if you have time. If not, tell the test administrator immediately.

Critical Attitude

Standardized tests are given to many students. Avoid searching for little-known facts or disagreeing with the basic ideas stated in the test. A standardized test is not looking for the odd answer. If you think you know the exception to the rule, don't apply it to a standardized test item.

Special Backgrounds

Students in the United States and Canada whose native language is not English have the biggest problem in standardized testing. They may be unfamiliar with the language the test uses and have few experiences in their backgrounds to help them understand the test situations in the items. Differences in environment cause problems even for students who have lived in the United States and Canada all their lives.

If you are not a native English speaker, seek help from your teacher and counselor. You may want to review samples of standardized tests before you take one. Perhaps the school can administer the test to you orally, if you understand better than you read.

No matter what problem you encounter with standardized tests, speak up. Help the tests work for you. That's what they are meant to do.

This section describes the many different types of questions and problems that appear on tests made up and given by your teacher.

Test Types	36
Test Formats	38
Test Items	40

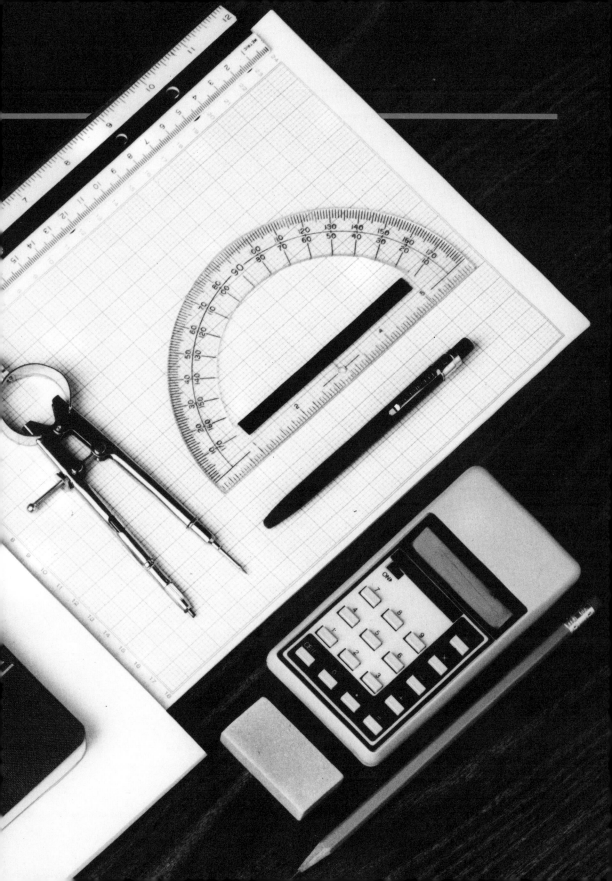

Teachers' Tests

T*eachers frequently make their own tests based on their lessons and class goals. They learn how to do so in courses they take while working toward their degree in education. Teachers also select tests made by educational publishers and sold to schools for their use. The four basic test types are pretests, diagnostic tests, instruction tests, and mastery tests.*

A fair teacher test stresses the learning areas that a teacher has emphasized during an instruction period. It also takes into consideration the learning level you should have reached when the test is given and provides enough testing time for you to do as well as you can.

Test Types

Pretests

Pretests are designed to provide information about you and your classmates before you begin instruction. They indicate what you know and can do. Because of this, they help your teacher in establishing a starting point for course work, planning lessons, and setting course goals. These tests do not count on your final grade directly, but they can help measure your achievement for a course when compared with a similar end-of-term test that shows what you have accomplished during the term. Many pretests and their end-of-term counterparts are teacher selected rather than teacher made.

Diagnostic Tests

While frequently given at the beginning of a course, diagnostic tests are also administered at other times. In fact, any time you have a learning problem, a diagnostic test may be advisable.

Diagnostic tests are designed to identify the reasons for a learning problem. For example, your teacher can make or select a diagnostic test to find out where you might be running into trouble with long division—a specific learning area. Since the test results would reveal where your trouble spots are, your teacher could plan lessons or drills to help you correct the situation.

On diagnostic tests, scores are helpful because they reveal which instructional goals are giving you difficulty. These tests do not count toward your grade.

Classroom Instruction Tests

Classroom instruction tests have several purposes. They measure achievement. They can be used as a teaching device. Written quizzes and oral question-and-answer sessions are examples of this kind of test. The answers are often discussed, and the discussion becomes a part of your instruction and learning process. Instruction tests usually count toward your grade. These are often designed by the teacher.

The chapter-end, unit-end, midterm, or final tests given both during a course and at its conclusion are also classroom instruction tests. Their results help teachers see how well you have achieved short-term and long-term goals. Teachers give these tests more than any other kind. The tests count toward your grade and are usually teacher made.

Mastery Tests

Mastery tests are used to measure the knowledge, skills, and other learning abilities students need to progress in school. Mastery tests help teachers find out when students are ready to progress, say, from beginning to intermediate algebra. When mastery tests are designed to reveal where pupils are having difficulty in specific areas, they are also diagnostic tests. Mastery tests usually count toward your grade and are usually teacher made.

Test Formats

Now that you have learned the basic types of teachers' tests, you should find out how they are designed. Teachers give tests in objective, essay, oral, and performance formats.

Objective Format

Objective tests are the most common kind of test given.

Objective tests are those in which you select or supply specific, short answers and in which scoring can be done with an answer key. When a teacher wishes to give an objective test, there are many choices among the kinds of questions that can be used. Common ones are: alternate-response (such as true-false questions), multiple-choice, fill-in, short-answer, and matching. Shown below is the same question presented in five different ways.

Examples:

1. *Alternate-response*
   The largest continent on earth is Asia. (T) F

2. *Multiple-choice*
   The largest continent on earth is
   a. Africa
   b. Asia√
   c. North America
   d. South America

3. *Fill-in*
   The largest continent on earth is <u>Asia</u>.

4. *Short-answer*
   What is the largest continent on earth?
   <u>Asia</u>

5. *Matching*

   Directions: Put the correct letter from Column B in front of each entry in Column A.

	Column A		Column B
<u>b</u>	Asia	a.	Location of earth's second longest river
<u>c</u>	Antarctica	b.	Largest continent on earth
<u>a</u>	South America	c.	Only continent with no permanent population

Objective tests are the most common kind of test given. There are several reasons for this. First, they are relatively easy to take. Second, your knowledge of a large amount of information can be tested in a short time. Up to forty items can be completed in most class periods, leaving more class time for instruction. Third, the scores of these tests are free of opinion because the answers are either right or wrong. This is why these tests are called objective tests. The fourth reason these tests are commonly used is that they take little time to score.

Essay Format

On essay tests, you express your answers in your own words. An essay item requires a relatively long answer and takes more time to score than an objective test. Essay tests focus on one or more of the following skills:

Essay tests call for giving answers in your own words.

1. How well you remember information
2. Your ability to organize and present information
3. Your ability to use information to come up with new ideas
4. Your ability to express yourself in writing

Oral Format

In some situations, oral tests are the best way to measure skills. Among these are your ability to express and organize your ideas or knowledge orally, to demonstrate your speaking skills, to pronounce and converse in another language, and to understand what you hear—which involves listening skills. When teachers decide to give oral tests, they select or make up the questions ahead of time.

Oral tests can take many forms. You may be required to prepare and give a report; then, you must answer questions about the subject of the report. Or, you may voluntarily answer questions orally in class. Another type of oral test may be where only you answer questions asked by one or more examiners.

In some oral tests, you write the answers. Many spelling tests are given this way. There are usually fewer questions in an oral test where the pupils are writing the answers, since students write more slowly than they speak.

Performance Format

Some classroom goals require you to develop the skills needed to produce a certain result, which you can also think of as a product. To evaluate your progress, the teacher must observe the steps you use to bring about the result. To do so, the teacher may use a performance test, which measures the quality of the skills themselves and the quality of the product. Skills that can be tested by performance include those required in classes such as speech, drama, physical education, driver education, art, and music. The solution to a mathematics problem or a project in industrial arts or home arts is also the product of a series of skills.

Teachers generally have a list of what you should be able to accomplish to achieve course goals that include the performance of a certain task. The list is called the teacher specifications. They can also be used as a guide for constructing performance tests. For example, a work-sample test in industrial arts might require you to complete a series of tasks set up at different stations. At each point, a part of the product is constructed or a particular skill is demonstrated. At the end, the completed product is evaluated, and the evaluation is your performance score.

Test Items

You will encounter many different types of test questions, or items, on teachers' tests. Each has its own preparation and answering strategies. Some items have special scoring methods you should know about. The rest of this section presents eleven common teacher-test items.

Alternate-Response Items

Alternate-response items are objective items that give a choice of two answers, but only one answer is right. Although most alternate-response items are true-false questions, there are other kinds. The following are examples of some of the varieties of alternate-response items:

1. 24 is a multiple of 2, 3, 4, 6, 8, and 12.   (T)   F
2. Is 24 a multiple of 2, 3, 4, 6, 8, and 12?   (Yes)   No
3. Is 24 a factor or a multiple of 12? (multiple)
4. The number 24 is a multiple of:
   a. 4   (T)   F   c. 9   T   (F)
   b. 6   (T)   F   d. 12   (T)   F

Preparing

Studying details and main ideas in outline form will help you prepare for alternate-response items. An outline can help you to identify relationships and to memorize any lists that are found in your unit of study. Flashcards can also help you memorize details and relationships.

Answering

Make sure that you understand how the answers are to be marked. Carefully read the directions for marking before you begin reading the questions. If these directions do not appear on the test, ask your teacher to explain them, if necessary.

Watch out for broad, general statements in each question. They have a tendency to be false unless words such as *usually, generally, sometimes,* or *often* appear. When these words are a part of the statement, it is likely to be true, but not always. In statements that are false, you may find words such as *always, never, none,* or *all.*

Read the statement carefully the first time. Your first reaction is important, and you want it to be based on an accurate reading. If you are sure you know the answer, follow the directions and mark your response.

When you are not quite sure of the answer but have a hunch, note it with a light check mark or a light plus or minus sign. Return to the lightly marked items after you have finished the test. You may have gotten hints from some of the questions that you answered. If you still do not know an answer, mark the item according to your first hunch.

If you draw a total blank, you may wish to guess. Do this only if the directions say "Mark all statements" or if the teacher has told you that there will be no penalty for guessing. If your directions are "Do not guess," don't.

A good true-false test will have answers organized in no regular pattern.

A good true-false test will have answers organized in no regular pattern, so do not spend time trying to figure one out. Do not be concerned if the same answer appears several times in a row. In most true-false tests, about one-half of the statements are true and one-half are false. This, however, is not a rule. Never change your answers just to equalize your trues and falses—you may change right answers to wrong ones.

Check your answers when you are finished to make sure you have marked items correctly. This can be done easily by reading the statement and applying your answer. For example, to check the following statement:

(T) F   Asia is the largest continent.

Say, "Yes, it is true that Asia is the largest continent." This kind of checking will help you avoid marking a statement incorrectly out of carelessness when you really know the right answer.

Multiple-Choice Items

The multiple-choice item is the most commonly used objective-type item. Depending on the teacher's goals and the subject, basic multiple-choice items usually consist of an incomplete statement or a question (the stem) followed by three or more possible choices. You must select the best choice. The incorrect choices are called distracters. They distract those students who are unsure about the answer.

The stem can also be in the form of a direction, the choices being possible results of correctly following the direction. Some multiple-choice items involve activities such as arranging entries in some kind of order.

Examples:

Question form: In which of the following states is the capital also the largest city?
a. Illinois b. Texas c. Massachusetts√ d. California

Incomplete statement form: The capital is also the largest city in
a. Illinois b. Texas c. Massachusetts√ d. California

In the examples above, there is one correct answer and three that are clearly wrong. Some multiple-choice items are designed to have you select the best answer from several that are possibly correct.

Example:

Which word best describes the study of plants?
a. biology   b. botany√   c. horticulture

Some multiple-choice items include, as one of the choices, "none of the above" or "all of the above." In this case, you must evaluate all the choices.

Example:

The set of factors of 24 is
a. [1, 2, 3, 4, 7, 12]   c. [1, 2, 3, 5, 8, 12]
b. [1, 2, 3, 4, 6, 8, 12]√   d. none of the above

Multiple-choice items can be difficult or easy, depending on how similar the choices are in meaning.

Examples:

Easy: What provides legal protection for an invention?
a. writ of habeas corpus
b. indictment
c. patent√

Harder: What provides legal protection for an invention?

a. copyright
b. patent√
c. warranty

Multiple-choice items can also ask you to make more than one choice. Time-ordering questions are an example of this.

Example:

Number the following events 1 through 4, in order from earliest to latest.

_2_	Truman Doctrine	_3_	Korean War
_4_	*Sputnik 1*	_1_	Atomic bomb dropped on Hiroshima

Preparing

As in most other types of tests, you will do your best work on a multiple-choice test if you are well prepared. Since multiple-choice items measure so many learning skills, you will want to review your subject matter thoroughly. All the preparation strategies such as outlining, flashcards, reading text material, participating in group study sessions, and taking part in classroom review will be helpful in preparing you to tackle the multiple-choice items successfully. The more familiar you are with the subject matter, the easier it will be for you to eliminate incorrect choices.

The more familiar you are with the subject matter, the easier it will be to eliminate incorrect choices.

Answering

Be sure to read the directions carefully before you mark any selections. Sometimes you are asked to give the correct answer. Sometimes, however, you are asked to choose the one best or worst answer. Some items require a choice of partly right or partly wrong answers, and some require more than one choice. Be sure you understand what you are looking for.

Follow the directions for marking. Some answers may be marked by underlining or checking the correct response. For others, you may have to circle numbers or letters that appear with the choices. On other tests, you will be asked to rearrange the choices in some kind of appropriate order. Or you may be asked to cross out all the wrong choices and leave only the correct one. Teachers may ask you to write your answers on a separate sheet of paper and leave the test unmarked. Whatever the answering method, do not let careless reading of directions lower your score.

Do not let careless reading of directions lower your score.

Here are three strategies for working the items on any multiple-choice test:

1. Look for answers that do not fit the stem. These are choices that can be eliminated because they are not grammatically or logically consistent with the stem.

2. Look for answers that are so precise and so carefully stated that they are probably correct.

3. Look for answers that are noticeably longer than the others. These are sometimes the correct choices because the teacher has had to include enough information to make them correct.

4. Examine the choices for guidance if you find the stem difficult to understand.

To answer a multiple-choice item that requires one choice, first read the statement or question carefully. Quickly go over the choices and mark the one you are sure is correct. Or, very lightly mark one you have a hunch about. Go through the list again and cross out any choices that you are sure are incorrect. This may help you eliminate distracters. Looking first for the correct answer and then crossing out the incorrect ones will make your list of possible choices smaller. Now, if you cannot choose the correct answer from the remaining choices, leave the question and come back to it later.

In a multiple-choice item that asks you to classify, place in the category (or categories) the answers you are certain about. Eliminate any answers that you know do not belong in the category. Return to the remaining answers and try to determine if they belong.

In items where you are to arrange a list of events chronologically, make a written list in the correct order in the margin of your test or on a piece of scratch paper. Then number each item. Write the numbers where they belong on your test.

Matching Items

A matching item usually has two lists of facts or principles.

A matching item is an objective item that usually has two lists of facts or principles. You are asked to match or pair each entry in the subject list (first list) with a word, symbol, phrase, or sentence in the response list (second list). Answers may be marked with numbers or letters. They are usually placed next to the entries in the first list, and the result is a row of answers.

Example:

Directions: Write the letter of the planet in Column 2 next to the words that describe the planet in Column 1.

	Column 1		Column 2
d	planet closest to the sun	a.	Earth
		b.	Pluto
c	largest planet	c.	Jupiter
b	farthest planet from the sun	d.	Mercury
		e.	Mars
a	third planet from the sun	f.	Venus

Answers can also be shown by drawing lines that connect the matched entries.

Example:

Directions: Draw a line from each color in Column 1 to the colors that can be mixed to produce it in Column 2.

Column 1	Column 2
pink	blue and green
green	blue and yellow
purple	red and white
orange	yellow and white
	red and yellow
	red and blue

Matching items can present a number of types of pairing: for example, famous people and their deeds; events and their dates; words or terms and their meanings; quotes and their sources; and objects and their categories. Sometimes opposites are matched, or similar entries. Cause and effect can also be matched.

The easiest matching items are those that use two columns. There are more difficult matching tests that use three or more columns.

Example:

Directions: Put the letters of each city's correct state and region, in that order, next to the name of the city.

	City	State	Region
C, e	1. Chicago	A. Florida	a. Northeast
E, b	2. Seattle	B. Arizona	b. Northwest
B, c	3. Tucson	C. Illinois	c. Southwest
A, d	4. Tampa	D. Vermont	d. Southeast
		E. Washington	e. Midwest
		F. Georgia	f. West

To prevent you from arriving at answers through the process of elimination, many matching items have unequal numbers of entries in the columns. In most tests, the subject column has fewer entries than the response column. Sometimes, whether the columns are even or not, the directions will state that answers may be used once, more than once, or not at all. This is another way to prevent you from guessing about leftovers.

Preparing

Because most matching exercises are designed to measure your recall of specific facts, your best preparation is daily reviewing with flashcards and outlining your notes. When studying for the test, memorize specific facts, rules, formulas, dates, and names of people and why they are important. Using your flashcards, make up practice matching questions. Make the fronts of the cards the subject column and the backs the response column. It is a good idea to organize your cards into subjects that go together in logical groupings, since your matching test is likely to be set up this way.

Outlining your notes is best done throughout your school term. If your notes are not already in outline form when your test is approaching, outline them right away. Then study the outline to see how information in your lessons relates.

If your notes are not already in outline form when your test is approaching, outline them right away.

Answering

When you read directions, make sure you understand how to indicate your choices—write the letter or number on the answer sheet, draw lines, or write your answers on a separate piece of paper. Note whether a choice may be used only once, more than once, or not at all.

Double-check to make sure that all of the responses appear on the page. Do not miss choices if, for some reason, the test is divided and part of it appears on the next page. Next, work down the subject column. Take each entry in turn. Choose the answers about which you are sure. Then work both columns in any order to complete your answers.

Many students do well going from the column that has the most information to the column with the least. In the following example, you would work from the left-hand column using that strategy. If you have trouble understanding what is required, reword your subject column so that the entries are questions. For the first entry in the example below, ask yourself, "Who invented the radio?"

Example:

Directions: Place in the blank next to each invention in Column A the letter of the inventor listed in Column B.

	Column A	Column B
e	1. invented the radio	a. Bell
h	2. invented the analog computer	b. Whitney
		c. Edison
c	3. invented the mimeograph	d. Morse
i	4. invented the reaper	e. Marconi
a	5. invented the telephone	f. Franklin
d	6. invented the telegraph	g. Howe
b	7. invented the cotton gin	h. Bush
		i. McCormick

Read each entry in the subject list and try to answer the question without looking at the choices. If you know the answer, read down the response list until you find it. If you cannot find the exact answer you thought of, try to find one that is similar or closely related and choose that one. As you go down the list writing those answers you are sure of in the blanks, also lightly write those you think you know. Go all the way through the list before you start again.

Now cross out the items in the response column that you have used, if you are sure they can be used only once. This will help you identify the choices that remain. Go back for your second round. Work on the entries you had hunches about. On your third round, go over the few remaining entries and choose probable matches.

Avoid changing answers. If you do your matching carefully in the first round, you will avoid getting into a situation where you have to go back and change one or more answers. Check all the answers by making a statement combining each subject entry with its matching response. For example, say to yourself, "Marconi invented the radio."

Avoid changing answers on matching items.

It is usually safe to guess on matching items if you must. Most matching exercises contain between five and fifteen items. Scoring formulas that count off for wrong answers are rarely used unless there is a large number of items. It is always wise to check the directions carefully, however. The danger of guessing on matching tests is greatest when the subject column and response column are even and each answer can be used only once. Then one wrong choice is really two or more wrong answers.

> *It is usually safe to guess on matching items if you must.*

Fill-In Items

Fill-in, or completion-type, items require you to supply the correct words, names, numbers, dates, or symbols missing from incomplete statements. There is usually a blank space provided within or next to the item. Fill-in items appear in many objective tests and can show up in a number of forms. In all forms, however, the answers are short and specific.

A. These items are incomplete statements with blanks within the sentences.

Examples:

1. The three branches of the U.S. government are the ___executive___ branch, the ___legislative___ branch, and the ___judicial___ branch.

2. "The world will little note nor long remember" is a phrase in a speech given by ___Abraham Lincoln___.

3. The first person to walk on the moon was ___Neil Armstrong___ in the year ___1969___.

B. In these items, a mathematics calculation has to be worked in order to complete a number sentence, or a mathematics principle has to be understood in order to give a correct answer without working out the problem.

Examples:
  1. $421 - 308 = \underline{113}$
  2. $6\,(2 + 3) = 6 \times 2 + \underline{6 \times 3} = \underline{30}$

Preparing

Make sure you know what will be covered on the test. Thorough study of the material, including outlining and taking time for thinking about what you are reading, will help prepare you to supply the information needed in this type of test. The most important kind of preparation is memorizing and understanding your material so you will be able to give the specific answers required.

Using your flashcards, devise a completion statement from each fact and make a practice test. If you have a study partner, you could make up a practice test for each other.

It is hard to bluff an answer on a fill-in item.

Answering

As in other tests, the directions must be carefully read and followed. In fill-in items, watch for instructions on how and where to mark your answers. If the item is in paragraph form, be sure to use capitalization for fill-ins that begin a sentence. Otherwise, you can lose points.

Because specific information is called for, it is hard to bluff an answer. You either know the information or not. If you know it, write it down. If you are not sure, but have a hunch, lightly write down your hunch and come back to it later. If all you still have is a hunch when you come back, go ahead and write it in.

Sometimes when you are reading through a fill-in item, many answers seem possible. If this happens, write them all down lightly and put a check by the one that seems best. Think about each one and cross out those that you realize are wrong or that do not fit so well as the others. If you still are not down to only one possible answer, finish the other items. Return to the incomplete one later. If you still are not sure then, write in the answer that you first checked.

The length of the blank may give you a clue. Sometimes, if two or more words are required, there will be a separate blank for each word.

Example:
The __Declaration__ of __Independence__ was written by Thomas Jefferson.

Most teachers, however, will try to avoid clues when they write their tests.

If you are unsure about what an item is asking, try to reword the statement in the form of a question.

Example:
One process of weathering is ___erosion___ .

What is one process of weathering?

When you know the idea of the required answer but have blanked out on the specific word, jot down the idea and any words that might mean the same as the one you cannot think of. Go on to other test items, and when you come back, chances are your memory will deliver the word you need. If not, write down the substitute word that you feel best supplies the answer. You may not receive full credit, but you have shown that you know what the item means.

Short-Answer Items

Short-answer questions require a brief response.

Like fill-in items, short-answer items are objective items that require you to supply an answer through the recall of information. The only difference is the form. A fill-in item is an incomplete statement. A short-answer item asks a question.

Fill-in item: Billions of small craters on the moon were caused by __meteoroids__ .

Short-answer item: What caused billions of small craters on the moon? meteoroids

Short-answer questions require a brief response. A list, a name, a date, a few words, and a short sentence are the kinds of answers to these items.

Preparing

Items of this type offer no choices, so you must be familiar with the subject in order to supply the correct answer. Your study for these questions must include a careful review of your classroom notes. The notes should give direction to your study. Go over any quizzes or homework papers you have in your reference file and become familiar with the types of questions your teacher tends to ask. Notice the kinds of answers your teacher expects and whether some of the answers are given partial credit if they are not entirely wrong.

Memorize names, dates, lists of information, definitions of terms, categories, and important principles that have been covered in your class. Try to connect each mathematics or science principle with an illustration. One way to do this is to draw or write an example of a principle in action. Do this on a flashcard. On the back of the card, write the name of the principle. Use these flashcards for your review. For example:

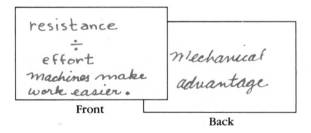

Front

Back

Answering

Read the directions carefully so that you understand exactly how and where your answers are to be written and the answer that is required. You will lose credit if you write correct information that does not answer the question being asked.

Example:

What is the property illustrated by the following example?

$6 (9 + 5) = (6 \times 9) + (6 \times 5)$

Answer from a student who read the question carefully: distributive

Answer from a student who did not read the question carefully: 84

Try to answer each question with the specific word, term, name, date, or other fact requested. In the case of mathematics questions, work any operations carefully and check your work. If test rules allow, answer the easy questions first.

When you are unsure of an answer, lightly jot down anything that might be close.

When you are unsure of an answer, lightly jot down anything you can think of that might be close. Go on to other questions. The correct answer may come to you, perhaps because something in the test jarred your memory. Do not give up on a question if, at first, you think you do not know the answer. Always go back. If you have studied, there will probably be some kind of answer you can give. Something is better than nothing. You may find that as you go over the hunches you wrote down, other ideas will occur to you.

If you find that two questions seem to be asking for the same answer, go back and reread the questions to make sure you did not misunderstand one of them. When you write your answers to short-answer items, make sure your handwriting is as easy to read as possible. Your teacher will appreciate not having to decode your answers. Some teachers will not give credit for an answer that cannot be read easily.

Essay-Test Items

An essay item asks you to explain, discuss, summarize, outline, or otherwise examine a topic and assemble the information into a logical pattern that you create. This item requires a longer answer than an objective-type item, and it cannot be scored with the kind of answer key used for objective tests. Essay questions are one type of free-response item: items in which you must supply the information. There are no choices given from which to select an answer. Fill-in and short-answer tests, plus many oral and performance tests, also have free-response items.

You will have much more freedom to respond on essay tests than on objective tests. You often have an opportunity to express your own ideas or to reach your own conclusions about the subject being discussed. Your answers can demonstrate your understanding of the subject matter in both broad terms and in detail.

There are several types of essay-test questions. These can be roughly grouped into two categories—extended-response and restricted-response items. Extended-response items are the type that allow you to organize your answers to best express your understanding of the subject.

Example:
> Discuss the role of the U.S. fleet in expanding the political influence of the United States in Asia in the early years of the 20th century.

Restricted-response items limit your answers. The limits might apply to length or the number of topics that may be included.

Example:
> Define *manifest destiny*. Give two examples of territorial acquisition credited to followers of this credo.

You may find that you are given a choice of questions to answer. For instance, there may be three questions from which you select one, or perhaps two, to answer. Essay tests are often given as open-book tests, which will be discussed later in this section. Some essay tests will have both extended-response and restricted-response items.

Preparing

Always find out if there will be essay items on a test. There are specific study methods you can use for essays that might not be necessary when preparing for a totally objective test.

The nature of an essay item calls for several specific skills. First, you must recall a great deal of information in order to answer the question correctly and properly discuss the required topic. Next, you should understand how the information fits together logically. Then, you need to know how to write about the information so that you communicate your knowledge. It is not enough to know—you must be able to show. Your reader has to understand what you mean. Correct punctuation, spelling, and other writing skills help you communicate your thoughts. As you study for essay tests, writing skills should be kept in mind and perhaps practiced.

To study for the recall of information, all of the study methods previously mentioned for other types of tests apply here. Try to establish a thorough knowledge of your subject. If your teacher likes essay-type questions, keep this in mind throughout the course in your daily review.

To effectively use your material, you will depend largely on your skill in organizing data and outlining. As you study for essay tests, outlining the material will help you see how ideas fit together. If you have been outlining all along in your daily review, go through your outlines and become familiar with the details that belong with each major head. Add more details that may occur to you. Read the outlines silently. Then read them aloud.

Try to imagine possible essay questions. Find examples in your textbook. Reword your major outline heads as if they were essay questions. Practice writing answers that include major ideas and a great many supporting details. Be concise and include as much relevant information as possible. Avoid including nonessential material.

Read what you have written in your practice answers. Have you said exactly what you mean? Is everything there that you wanted to include? If possible, have someone else

When preparing, try to imagine possible essay questions.

read your answer and try to spot omissions. Listen to any suggestions about your writing style. Go back and check any previous tests where your teacher wrote comments on your essays.

Answering

The most important thing to know about an essay question is what is expected in the answer. Because an essay question deals with topics that require more information than merely a word, symbol, or number, you must be sure of what it specifically requires. Does it say "explain," "discuss," "analyze"? Does it ask a specific question? It is a waste of your valuable test-taking time to write about material that does not belong in your answer.

Reading Directions. Exactly what is wanted should be clearly stated in the directions. Some tests will have one set of general directions that apply to the entire test as well as specific directions for each test section or item. Read and follow all of them carefully.

General directions might include: how you are to write your answer; whether you should use pen or pencil; whether you should use one side of the paper or both sides; where you should write your name; where your answers should be written; how much time you should spend; and whether you are to answer all the questions. If the directions include a limit on the number of words the answers may be in length, such as 100 to 150 words, ask your teacher how to estimate the number of words you will write.

Specific directions for individual items may also include word lengths. While you are reading directions, underline all the important words and phrases that tell you how the questions should be answered and what should be included. Some of the words might be: *explain, state, summarize, outline, compare, prove,* and *illustrate*. Once you have identified these instructions, you must be careful to follow them in your answers. Here are explanations of ways to follow specific direction words:

Good scores on essay questions may depend on how well you have followed the directions.

Explain	Tell about and show how, using an illustration, if possible.
State	Briefly express ideas, but do not go into much detail or illustration.
Summarize	Bring together the main points without going into a lengthy discussion or presenting much detail.
Outline	Present the information in outline form that shows the relationship of broad topics (major heads) to specific information (details).
Compare	Write comparisons showing similarities. Some questions also ask for dissimilarities.
Prove	Write a discussion of arguments that favor the statement. At times it is also helpful to discuss those arguments that take the opposite point of view.
Illustrate	Give the best example you can think of. Do not define or discuss.

Remember how important it is to keep your writing focused on the specific words that tell you how to answer the essay question. Good scores may depend on how well you have followed the directions.

Preparing to Write. Read through all the questions carefully before you do any writing. Estimate the amount of time you will have for each. Sometimes your teacher will tell you how much time to spend on each item. In planning your time, be sure to allow a few minutes for checking, proofreading, or handling difficult questions.

If there are choices to be made about which questions you will answer, choose before you start answering any. Circle or check the questions you can best answer. If possible, choose questions that are related in some way. What you write about one may reveal ideas about topics to cover in another. Only answer the number of questions called for in the directions. If you are to answer three out of five, choose only three. If the directions say answer the first question and any other two, be sure to answer the first question.

Writing. When you are sure that you understand the directions, follow these suggestions to begin your answering strategy:

1. Outline your answer or organize your ideas in a numbered list. Jot your ideas down lightly in the margin or somewhere on your paper. This helps your work to be well organized.

2. If your teacher permits, underline important names or ideas as you write. This will point out that you recognize their importance.

3. Where you can, use an illustration, such as a sketch or a diagram, to demonstrate your understanding of the subject.

4. Use original illustrations as examples. Try to avoid using the same ones that were used in your classwork.

5. Include statistics where appropriate. These can be shown in a graph, chart, or table.

6. Do not clutter up your answer with unnecessary information.

7. Check with the teacher to see if you may leave a space between your paragraphs. The space will make your work more legible.

8. Emphasize quality rather than quantity. Do not pad your answers unless you are adding important material.

If permitted, use scratch paper for your outline, to make notes, to work problems, and to try out sketches. As you are writing, ideas may begin to come to you too fast for you to get them all down in detail. Quickly jot the main points down elsewhere so you will not forget them.

In each paragraph, try to discuss only one main idea. This should be easy to do if you have made an outline. Write your main idea as the topic sentence and then finish the paragraph with details, examples, illustrations, and other information that supports the main idea.

Throughout your essay answer, use the vocabulary you have learned in the course to express yourself. Each subject has its own special terminology. Make a point of using the words that best communicate the subject matter.

When expressing opinions, give reasons for them. An opinion should be backed up by your reasons for arriving at it. Writing with examples telling why you like or dislike or agree or disagree with something is much more convincing than merely stating that yes, you agree or like something, or no, you do not agree or like something. Besides, your reasons are probably the most important part of your answer.

Stick to the question. If you do not know the answer, do not try to bluff by writing about something else. If you are unsure of an answer but have a hunch about it, try writing out your hunch instead of giving no answer at all. You may get some credit, which is better than getting no credit.

Write all the information that is needed to answer the question. Do not leave something out because you assume that the teacher is aware that you know it. Even if your teacher is aware that you know something, you should show how well you can relate it to other material.

Use the vocabulary you have learned in the course to express yourself.

If, for one reason or another, you answer more questions than necessary, pick the best ones to satisfy the required total and cross out the rest. If only three questions of five are required, for example, your first three might be the only ones graded, and those might not be your best answers.

If you are running out of time and have not finished, quickly outline answers for the rest of the items you are working on and the remaining required questions still unanswered. You may not receive full credit, but you will probably get some. It is possible that your teacher may like your outlined answers and give you full credit. Some teachers actually prefer outlines to long-winded discussions.

Leave some space at the end of your answer to each question. If something occurs to you while answering another question, then there will be room to write additional material.

Some teachers care less than others about spelling and writing style. You, however, should present all your work in the best possible manner. Take pride in how your papers look. Your answers make a much better impression if they are written neatly with attention paid to correct spelling and punctuation.

When you are finished writing your answers, go back and read them again. Watch for careless errors such as skipped words or misspellings. You also may find that you have left out important information that you wanted to include.

Scoring

When teachers write essay items, they have ideal answers in mind. Many teachers write down a list of important points that they would like to see included in the answer. Other teachers make outlines. In either case, they have something with which to compare each answer.

Example:

Question: Name three major water pollutants.
Discuss how each is introduced into waterways; what harm it does; and what can be done to correct the problem.
Teacher's list of important points:
topsoil from erosion
industrial wastes
sewage
detergents
thermal pollution
pesticides

Some teachers take off points for sloppy writing, misspelled words, and grammatical errors. If they do not take off points for these things, they may mark all of the errors in order to bring them to your attention. Sometimes separate scores will be given: one for the information and one for writing mechanics.

Some teachers assign a specific number of points for each test question. They may have a five-point scale with a letter grade assigned to each point value: 5-A; 4-B; 3-C; 2-D; 1-F. The teacher evaluates the answer to each question and assigns it a score. There is a reason for the score an answer receives. One teacher's scale is shown below:

Score	Letter Grade	Evaluation
5	A	Answer includes most information required. Excellent organization. Shows student understands the material very well.
4	B	Good answer, but incomplete in some way. Misses a major point here or there.
3	C	Shows minimum effort and little basic understanding. Focus is off the mark. Just gets by.
2	D	Poor—too much padding and too little knowledge or understanding of the material.
1	F	Nothing here that indicates student knows the material.

Some teachers use the sorting method for grading essay tests.

For long essay answers, some teachers use the sorting method. In this method, the teacher reads all the answers quickly and sorts them into five piles—one for each grade. If an answer does not fit into a particular pile after the first reading, the teacher puts it in the pile that seems closest. For instance, if the teacher is not sure whether the answer deserves a B or a C, but thinks that it might be a C, the answer will be marked with a question and put in the C pile. Then the answers are read a second time. Those marked with a question mark will be given particular attention. During this second reading, some of the papers may be switched to another pile. The score or letter grade assigned is based on the pile in which the paper finally remains.

Open-Book Test Items

To answer an open-book item, you will use reference materials—books or notes. Some open-book tests are given in the classroom. Others are homework assignments.

Studies have shown that open-book tests can be as reliable as other kinds of tests. Good students usually get high grades, and poor students still tend to get low grades. As a matter of fact, good students usually have an advantage because they are more familiar with the reference materials and may be better readers. Poor students, on the other hand, read more slowly and have more trouble locating answers.

Preparing

There is little difference between study methods for open-book tests and study for any other kind of exam. The more you know and understand the subject matter, the better you will do on any test. It is a good idea, however, to become particularly familiar with reference materials. The sooner you can locate the information you need, the more time you will have to write a good, complete answer.

It is a mistake to think that you do not have to study for an open-book test. Many open-book questions deal with broadly defined ideas and principles. You need to recognize and understand an idea before you can intelligently select isolated facts and other supporting details to illustrate it. If you have not read or thought about the material beforehand, too much of your test-taking time will be used trying to figure out what the question means.

Answering

Be careful to follow the test directions exactly. With references at your disposal, you want to be sure that you come up with the information your teacher has asked for. Do not relax to the point of carelessness because you can look up information. Stay alert to the focus of the question and how the directions instruct you to answer it. Read the question carefully and as many times as necessary so that you understand exactly what is required.

For Objective Items. Locate your material first. If you are being tested on material found in a particular section of a book, put index cards or paper strips as bookmarks at the beginning and end of the section. If you have trouble finding a specific word or answer, check the index or glossary. Read the headings and subheadings in the contents and chapters to find the general area where specific information might be found. Check chapter-end material and the introduction to locate the chapter where a specific piece of information is discussed.

Review the directions. Be sure you clearly understand how the answers are to be given. Follow the directions exactly. If you have time when you have finished, go over the test items again and check to make sure you gave the answers you meant to give.

For Essay Items. Read the question carefully and think about it for a while. When you understand it, begin to construct an outline. Jot down relevant topics and names. Use this outline to find references in the index or table of contents of your book. Mark the page reference next to the entry in your outline so you do not have to keep going back to the index. Do not neglect to check illustrations for additional information.

It is a mistake to think that you don't have to study for an open-book test.

Stay with the focus of the question. Using your book, notes, and anything else allowable, construct a more complete outline of the material, including details. Try to organize the information in a logical way. Go back to the discussion of essay items in this section and again read how to organize an essay. When you are satisfied that you have the basic outline completed and you know how to write an essay, prepare a first draft of your answer.

Read the draft over, checking for spelling, complete sentences, and general writing style. Check particularly to be sure that your essay answers the question exactly and in your own words. It is a bad idea to copy paragraphs from the textbook. It is better to rephrase all information.

Because you have had the information available during the test, your teacher may be unwilling to give much credit for incomplete or poorly organized answers. Your teacher may expect more from you for answers to open-book questions and may grade the tests more strictly. Careful attention to neatness, grammar, spelling, and directions will present your work in its best form and could swing a doubtful score to a better one.

Performance Test Items

A performance test is just that—a performance where you physically show whether you can do something skillfully and, in some cases, safely. While other tests show what you know, performance tests show what you know and whether you can demonstrate that knowledge in a presentation of some sort. Sometimes, the outcome of a performance test is a product of some sort. The product, plus how skillfully you worked and how well you followed the correct procedures in order to make it, are all evaluated.

Preparing

Your textbook and class notes are your best resources for study of the facts and principles involved in performance testing. Practice is your best preparation for presentation. It is important in either case to be clear about your teacher's expectations.

Practice is your best preparation for performance tests.

If you have been paying attention from day to day, you should have some idea of the areas that your teacher has emphasized. In classes such as industrial arts, auto mechanics, home arts, and driver education, one important area will probably be safety. Review all of the safety rules you have been taught and prepare to follow them in your presentation.

In business education, certain skills such as typing and shorthand are evaluated on the basis of speed. Practice is your study method here. For these and other business skills, such as calculator operations and computer programming, accuracy is essential as well as speed. Again, knowledge of the instrument is important, and practice is necessary to increase your skills.

In some areas, such as art and music, your daily work is both your practice and your study. What you learn as you create a piece of sculpture shows up in your next piece.

Your physical and mental training as you practice a piece of music accumulates and increases your skill each time you go through your routine of scales, steps, fingering exercises, or vocalizing. Your best study is to follow a daily discipline set up by you and your teacher.

For some oral performance tests, you may require a rehearsal. This practice time will help you identify areas that need work. You will have a chance to polish up the rough spots before you present yourself for the test. If possible, tape your speech, role, or report. Listen to yourself and try to evaluate your performance, making notes where necessary. Go over your notes and practice again. Listening to yourself or having someone listen to you will help you pinpoint your strong and weak points.

Tape-record your speech, role, or oral report.

Practice the speech, role, or report until you know it thoroughly. Even if you can refer to notes for a speech or are reading a report, practicing in front of a mirror, for a family member, or on tape will help build your confidence. One thing that can make you nervous is being ill-prepared.

Presenting

The directions on a performance test, whether given orally or in writing, will state what you are to do and what you will have to work with for your presentation. If you are being asked to identify parts of something, be sure you understand how the identifications are to be made. Do you give the name of the part, its use, or both?

When producing a work sample, make sure you understand the problem before you begin to work. The directions should tell you clearly how to go about the tasks and in what order each task is to be performed. Always keep safety procedures in mind. You also should be aware of any time limits.

In some performance tests, the directions are particularly vital to success. There are situations where doing things out of their specified order will cost you points. Many driving examiners, for example, will count off points if you do not buckle your seat belt before starting the car.

Take extra time to be sure you understand everything you need to know about what to do during the performance test and how to do it. Follow the directions exactly. Perform your tasks as closely as possible to the ideal procedures that you have learned in order to demonstrate your skills.

This kind of test may make you nervous, but try to overcome the jitters by focusing your thoughts and energies away from whoever is watching and toward your desired results. Once you get involved in your performance task, your confidence is likely to assert itself.

Scoring

Many performance tests are scored with the help of a check list. The teacher has a list of all the skills and procedures that are to be evaluated and uses it for all students taking the test.

Check lists might state, in order, each individual step in a process, each safety measure expected to be taken, or each skill that is being measured. When you see how your check list has been marked, you have the details of how you did on the test.

A rating scale, where each item on the check list is given a value of from 0 to 4, for example, can be used to assign a score to your performance. Rating scales can be adapted to evaluate the finished article as well as the manner in which it was made or accomplished. Some teachers assign scores based on the percentage of items checked on the check list.

In some areas, such as handwriting, drawing, craft projects, shop projects, and home arts projects, where a product is created, your teacher may use a quality scale to compare your work with the work of others or with an established standard. A quality scale consists of eight or ten samples taken from the collection of the articles being evaluated. These samples are chosen to represent different rankings in quality. They are put in order from best to worst and are used as comparison models for your work, which is assigned the ranking of the sample that most nearly matches your work in quality.

Oral Test Items

Oral tests are given and/or taken orally. They can be administered to a group or an individual. Some are performance tests. These include speeches, oral reports, interviews, and recitations. For oral performance tests, you have a good idea of the exact tasks required of you beforehand. For other oral tests, you generally do not know the exact questions before you are tested.

When you need to prepare for an oral performance test, review the information on performance tests in this section. The information presented here will briefly discuss other oral tests, which may be identical in format to many of the written tests you have already learned about. When you know your oral test items are going to be alternate-response, multiple-choice, or short-answer questions, for example, make sure to review those parts in this section.

Oral tests can combine performance items and other test items. For example, you may be required to give a report and then answer questions the teacher or class thought of as you presented the report. To prepare for these tests, review this portion along with the appropriate information presented earlier in the section.

Preparing

First, find out as much as you can about the material that will be covered on the test. Study your material as you would for a written test. However, practice giving answers orally. This will get you used to hearing yourself express the information aloud and lessen the possibility of nervousness.

Answering

The teacher may give questions orally that you answer orally, or you may answer in writing. Sometimes, the teacher will give you written questions that you answer orally. If the directions are given orally, listen for instructions on how and where you are to answer. Pay attention to any questions given orally to other students and to the answers

Pay attention to questions given orally to other students and to the answers they give.

they give. Let your mind become involved with the subject matter.

Before you begin any oral test, you must understand exactly what is expected of you. For oral questions, use your listening skills. It is important not to miss the point of questions. This is easily done if you are a poor listener. Ask questions if you are not clear about the kind of answer your teacher wants.

Do not blurt out disorganized information if you answer orally. Think a few moments and try to organize your answer. Never answer, "I do not know," if you can avoid doing so. It is highly unlikely that you have never heard about the topic. Rather, begin to answer with whatever relevant information you do know. Information may occur to you as you speak. Your teacher may ask you some additional questions that will help lead you to a more complete answer.

Never answer "I do not know" if you can avoid doing so.

Scoring

Oral tests with written answers are scored like other written tests. If your teacher does not use a sound tape or videotape to record your oral answers, they will be scored while you are answering. As in performance tests, your teacher will use some kind of check list—and sometimes a rating scale—as a guide for marking whatever is being evaluated. Some teachers mark each item with a $\overset{+}{\sqrt}$ for excellent, a $\sqrt{}$ for good, and a $\overset{-}{\sqrt}$ for less than good. Some teachers simply mark each item "pass" or "did not pass."

Mathematics Word Items

Mathematics word items usually require more than one or two calculations. They present a situation that needs solving. For example, the word item could involve an accounting exercise or a practical application of a mathematics principle to everyday life.

Preparing

Keep a file of mathematics quizzes, homework, and class-work. Go over all the word problems, checking for errors and ways you may have misread the questions. Also, check for places where you were careless. Rewrite a number of problems using different quantities. Solve and check the problems. Memorize any formulas or rules that apply to the material being tested. Practice several examples using the formulas.

Answering

Your test directions should tell you where you are to do your figuring, how and where the answer should be written, whether your proofs should be included, and how much time you have. Some of these directions may be given orally, so be sure to pay close attention to what your teacher tells you.

The basic approach to any mathematics word item is to use what is known to find what is unknown.

The basic approach to any mathematics word item is to use what is known to find what is unknown. As you read each problem, underline or jot down the given data. The two typical examples that follow will be analyzed so that you can see how to work them out and how to check your answers. They will establish your foundation for working all test items of this type.

Example 1:

Lydia shopped for a new coat and found one on sale. The original price was $140. The coat was marked 30 per cent off. What was the sale price?

In this example, you know the original price and the percentage marked off for the sale.

$140 × 30 per cent = $42

Is $42 the answer? No. You must now subtract the amount marked off from the original price. $140 less $42 = $98. The sale price is $98.

Even if you had stopped with $42, you could have quickly discovered your error by checking.

Check: Coat originally cost $140. Sale discount is 30 per cent. Sale price is 70 per cent of original price (100 per cent less 30 per cent); 70 per cent of 140 is 98.

Example 2:

Abner needs to order wallpaper for his bedroom. The paper he likes comes in rolls 18 inches, or $1\frac{1}{2}$ feet, wide and 24 feet long. He must buy the wallpaper in complete rolls. How many rolls must he buy?

In this problem, what is known is the information giving the dimensions of Abner's four walls. They are 8-by-12-foot rectangles. You also know that the dimensions of the door and the window will have to be accounted for. Another known quantity is the size of each wallpaper roll. Using this information, you must find the total amount of wall-paper that he needs to use. You use the given dimensions to do so.

For this kind of problem, it is extremely helpful to sketch the walls with the wallpaper widths, as shown. In this way, you can figure how many widths are needed to fill a wall, how many widths of 8-foot length make a roll, and how many rolls are needed for each room. Then you can add the total amount of wallpaper needed in terms of rolls and figure the needed amount. If there is a remainder in your figuring that represents a partial roll, an extra roll must be purchased.

First, then, obtain all the information you can from the known quantities:

North wall If you divide 12 feet by $1\frac{1}{2}$ feet (the width of the wallpaper), you find that the wall will hold 8 widths. Since each wall is 8 feet long, you will need 64 feet, or $2\frac{2}{3}$ rolls.

East wall The door is 3 feet across, which will take 2 widths of wallpaper. The needed length for this area would have been 2 times 6 (2 widths times 6 feet), or 12 feet, which equals $\frac{1}{2}$ roll. Therefore, the east wall needs $\frac{1}{2}$ a roll less than a full wall, or $2\frac{1}{6}$.

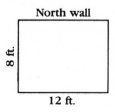

North wall

8 ft.

12 ft.

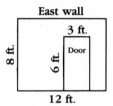

East wall

3 ft.

Door

8 ft.

6 ft.

12 ft.

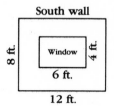

South wall

8 ft.

Window

4 ft.

6 ft.

12 ft.

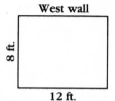

West wall

8 ft.

12 ft.

South wall   The window is 6 feet across, which will take 4 widths of wallpaper. The needed length for this area would have been 4 times 4 (4 widths times 4 feet), or 16 feet, which equals $\frac{2}{3}$ of a roll. Therefore, the south wall needs $\frac{2}{3}$ of a roll less than a full wall, or 2 rolls.

West wall   The same is required as for the north wall, or $2\frac{2}{3}$ rolls.

The total number of rolls needed to cover the four walls turns out to be $9\frac{1}{2}$. So Abner will have to buy 10 rolls.

Check: To find the total wall space in square feet to be covered, multiply 8 feet times 12 feet times 4 feet. The answer is 384 square feet. Subtract 24 square feet for the window and 18 square feet for the door. There are 342 square feet of walls to be covered.

To find the total square footage of wallpaper to be used, multiply $1\frac{1}{2}$ times 24 times $9\frac{1}{2}$ (number of rolls). The answer is 342 square feet in $9\frac{1}{2}$ rolls of wallpaper.

This checks your accuracy, but remember that the answer to the question is 10 because Abner must buy complete rolls of wallpaper.

Each mathematics word item you encounter will have its own proper procedure for solving and checking answers, but there are some basic strategies you can always use. Many of these strategies also apply to other types of mathematics problems.

1. Read the problem carefully so you clearly understand what you are trying to find.

2. Jot down all of the information, including any formulas, that you are given or that you know applies to the operations in the problem.

3. Estimate an answer, if possible, before you begin, and check your final answer against the estimate.

4. Where they are helpful, make sketches.

5. Use all the relevant information that you find in the stated problem to find needed information (as in the second example, where you used the width dimensions of the walls in the room to determine how many wallpaper widths would fit on one wall).

6. If you are stuck working a problem one way, start from another angle (as in the check in the first example).

7. Where a problem is given in symbols, work it out using small numbers so you can easily check your procedure.

Some additional strategies to remember are:

1. Do not try to add apples and oranges. Make sure your units are the same or in the same system.

2. Do neat work. This helps your teacher as well as you. If you are neat, you will not make careless errors based on misreading your own numbers. Also, when you check your answer, any errors will be easier to find on a neat paper.

3. If you run out of time, you may get credit for problems you have not finished if you outline the procedures you would use to solve them.

4. Check your work. Does it come reasonably close to your estimated answer? Does it make sense? Is the answer expressed in the correct units? If you suspect an answer may be wrong, work it again, if time permits. Use the checking procedures you know for each operation.

Graph, Table, and Chart Items

Become familiar with the basic types of graphs, tables, and charts.

Graphs, tables, and charts are devised to present a large amount of information in a convenient form. When you learn how to read them, you can see certain relationships or trends more easily than by looking at a list of statistics or reading a lengthy description. Because they are so handy in research and study, your teachers will, from time

Bar graph:

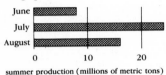

summer production (millions of metric tons)

Line graph:

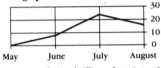

summer production (millions of metric tons)

Pictograph:

June   July   August

summer production (millions of metric tons)

Circle graph:

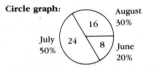

summer production (millions of metric tons)

to time, give you exercises in reading and interpreting these devices.

Become familiar with the forms of graphs, tables, and charts. There are four kinds of graphs: bar graphs, line graphs, pictographs, and circle graphs.

Tables vary in size and complexity. They contain numbers, words, or other items in columns and lines. Charts can consist of a list, diagram, picture, or table. The words *table* and *chart* are sometimes used interchangeably.

Preparing

Review the graphs, tables, and charts here and in your textbooks and classwork. Your mathematics text may have a chapter on graphs and charts that can help you in your review.

Practice constructing graphs, tables, and charts. Use information from any book. This practice will help you become more familiar with the parts of these devices, how they are labeled, and how information can be shown.

Answering

Your directions will tell you how to answer the questions. Each question must be carefully read so that you will locate the correct data with which to answer it. Be sure you are clear about what is being asked in questions.

Next, take a careful look at the graph, table, or chart. Make sure you know what data are shown. Check the labels or headings. Read the title. If there is no title, try to think of a good one. Stating a title can bring the purpose of a graph, table, or chart into focus. What would be an appropriate title for Graph 1?

Graph 1

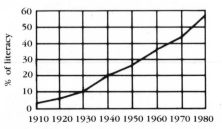

One good title might be "Growth in literacy, 1910–1980."
Now practice answering with two questions typical of these
types of items. Study Graph 1 and use it to find your answers.

1. What percentage of the population could read in
   1930?

2. How many people could read in 1940?

Could you answer both questions from the information on
Graph 1? No, only Question 1 can be answered directly
from the data. To answer Question 2, you need to know
the total population in 1940. In this case, you can use the
graph to arrive at your answer only if you are given or can
obtain additional information.

For graphs, always keep in mind what the labels on
the axes, or horizontal and vertical lines, mean. You must
also be clear on the units of measurement being used—as,
for example, the dates or number intervals. On the vertical
axis of Graph 1, each mark represents 10 per cent; on the
horizontal axis, each mark represents 10 years.

Some graphs are drawn with more than one line. The
lines may be of different types—solid, dotted, or broken—
or of different colors. Other graphs contain bars that have
variations within each bar. These variations can also be
shown with different patterns or colors. Make sure when
you are answering a question that you are following the
right line or color.

When your test requires you to make a graph, remember to bring a ruler and any other necessary supplies.
Follow the directions exactly. Do your work in convenient
units so that your graph is a manageable size and can be
read easily.

Understanding the headings and other parts of tables
and charts is important for tests requiring interpretation of
these devices. If you need to make tables and charts, bring
supplies, if necessary.

Graphs can be quite complex, having several lines and bars.

Energy sources

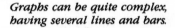

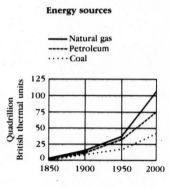

Income and outlays

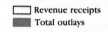

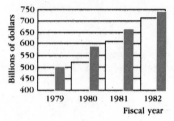

IV STANDARDIZED TESTS

*This section describes and analyzes
standardized tests. The major types
of test items are reviewed.*

Test Goals	78
Two Testing Methods	79
Five Test Categories	79
Standardized Test Guidelines	81
Test Quality	84
Test Development	85
Test Administration	89
Test Items	89

Standardized Tests

The creation of standardized tests is a highly specialized area of educational psychology. One of the functions of education psychologists is to organize information about learning. The variety in types of standardized tests shows how complex learning is.

Test Goals

Community Reporting

When schools give standardized tests, they have three goals. One is to report to your community about the progress of the students in area schools. Sometimes this reporting is called accountability.

Curriculum Evaluation

Another goal is for the school to use test results to identify strengths and weaknesses in the courses taught. If the standardized test selection process used by the schools includes procedures to ensure that what is being taught is what the standardized test is measuring, then test scores can be used to show how well the curriculum is developed. The test results for your school may identify strong and weak points in the educational plan.

Student Progress

A third goal of standardized testing is to help you, the student, relate your abilities and achievements to those of other students across the country or to evaluate how well you are progressing toward certain goals or standards. This information can help you make plans for future study and for your career. Using test results, teachers and counselors can help you make these plans.

Two Testing Methods

Group Tests

Most standardized tests are group tests; that is, they are given, or administered, to groups. These groups may include a large number of people. The tests rely heavily on your ability to read and write. There is little opportunity for you to receive individual help during the test period.

Individual Tests

Some standardized tests are given individually—to one person at a time—sometimes by a trained examiner. These tests are often given to children in the primary grades who cannot yet read and write. The examiner may use many visual aids such as pictures, puzzles, posters, and objects of different sizes, shapes, and colors. The examiner follows a highly detailed set of instructions. These are used both in presenting materials and in evaluating responses.

Five Test Categories

To help bring standardized testing into focus for you, five general categories are discussed in detail here. These categories are (1) learning ability tests, (2) aptitude and interest tests, (3) achievement tests, (4) competency tests, and (5) personality tests. These tests are generally available for all age groups, from kindergarten through college. They are discussed briefly below in terms of their general use. Keep in mind as you read about these tests that the ones you take may have different names. But most of them can be placed into one of the five categories.

Learning Ability Tests

Learning ability tests are designed to measure the knowledge and skills you have acquired and how well you use these skills at the time of the test. These tests may try to

Learning ability tests are sometimes called intelligence tests, mental ability tests, academic aptitude tests, or scholastic aptitude tests.

discover your special abilities and thought processes to predict your potential for future learning.

Learning ability tests are sometimes called intelligence tests, mental ability tests, academic aptitude tests, or scholastic aptitude tests. Many learning ability tests report an intelligence quotient (IQ) score.

Aptitude and Interest Tests

Aptitude tests, which sometimes include interest sections, are designed to show your potential ability to perform a certain type of activity. The results may also predict that you may have difficulty doing some types of activities.

Achievement Tests

The standardized test you are most likely to take in school is the achievement test. This test is planned to find out how much you have learned. It may cover only one subject, such as reading. However, the achievement tests most often given have many sections, which are called batteries. The batteries cover different subjects. Reading and mathematics are almost always part of standardized achievement tests. Language usage, social studies, spelling, and science are often included, also.

Standardized diagnostic tests are individualized achievement tests given to help meet students' special needs. Suppose you have taken a standardized group achievement test and a learning abilities test. Results show you have a high level of learning ability. Your results from the general achievement test are also high in most areas. However, some scores from the language section are low. Your teacher may suggest that you take one or more standardized diagnostic tests, which are designed to find the nature of your learning problem. A number of well-researched practice materials have been developed to help correct problems identified by these tests.

Competency Tests

Competency tests are another special kind of achievement test. They are categorized separately because they can be critical in your educational progress. They are designed to show that when you complete school, you are prepared to perform the basic tasks you need to function in society. Not all schools have competency tests, but many do. You should find out if you will be required to take competency tests in your school.

A competency test measures your mastery of a specific subject or set of skills. Schools often require that these tests be completed with a passing score before you move to a different level.

Personality Tests

Personality tests are different from other standardized tests. They most often are designed to help you identify how you feel about yourself and others—those feelings that can help or hinder your progress in school, at home, or in a career.

Standardized Test Guidelines

There are general principles of standardized testing that should be followed in order for the tests to provide accurate measures. All standardized tests should be carefully designed and administered in the following ways:

1. No matter what kind they are, standardized tests should always be given under the same conditions to all those who take them. The tests should be given with the same directions, the same time for answering, and the same test-room conditions. The students taking the tests should be able to hear the directions and have the same opportunity for undisturbed concentration.

2. Standardized tests should be prepared by people who are testing experts. These people are called psychometrists. They have years of experience in developing standardized tests.

3. Standardized test materials should be extensively researched and tried out experimentally before being used on a test.

4. The fourth guideline involves two terms with which you may be unfamiliar: norm referencing and criterion referencing. These are two kinds of standards by which your standardized test results can be compared. It is probable that you have taken both norm-referenced and criterion-referenced standardized tests. Although these standards may sound complicated, they are easy to understand. All results for a standardized test should be compared to a single standard.

Standardized tests should always be given under the same conditions to all those who take them.

Norm Referencing

The results of a norm-referenced test give you a specific placement among others who have taken the test. They help schools report to the community about their progress in relation to other schools and often provide an accountability report to the community.

A norm is an average. In standardized testing, a norm is an average achieved on a test by an experimental sample group. The sample group is chosen when tests using this kind of standard are being made. The choice of who will be in a norm group is an important part of standardized test preparation.

If your test results are going to be compared to the results of a norm group, the individuals in that group will have to be as representative as possible of you and all the other students who will take the test. Norm groups should include a variety of ethnic and racial backgrounds. They should also include students with a range of ages and a proportion of sexes equal to the group of students taking the test.

Criterion Referencing

Criterion-referenced tests help teachers discover your strengths and weaknesses, as well as the appropriateness of the classroom materials you have been studying. Results of these tests can be used for community accountability reports when a strong relationship has been established between the tests and community educational goals. The items used in the tests are developed to show your understanding and skills in a variety of subjects including mathematics, reading, language, social studies, and science.

On criterion-referenced tests, your results are not compared to the results of a norm group but rather to a set of objectives. Each of these is called a criterion. This standard is specific. It is related to learnings that you will have to show you have attained.

To begin your understanding of criterion-referenced tests, it would be useful for you to compare them to teachers' tests. Most teachers' tests are criterion referenced. That is, your teacher—say in English—decides that for a test you will have to know what declarative, interrogative, imperative, and exclamatory sentences are. You will receive 25 points for each type of sentence that you know. The test questions are built around measuring your understanding of these four types of sentences. Whether the rest of the class knows them does not matter. You are expected to show your knowledge of the sentence types.

On many standardized criterion-referenced tests, individual scores for each subject are reported. Many teachers like these tests because they can use results of this type to set course goals. If, for example, 75 per cent of your class misses questions about decimals, then your teacher can plan your mathematics course with emphasis on decimals.

Often the test report also shows the performance of the class and the school system. The report may further give the proportion of students correctly answering each item on the samples taken as the test was developed.

Test Quality

The quality of a standardized test can be measured by three major standards: (1) validity, (2) reliability, and (3) practicality. Any standardized test must be valid, reliable, and practical to be useful.

Any standardized test must be valid, reliable, and practical to be useful.

Validity

A test is valid depending on how well it measures what it is intended to measure. For example, a test of reading comprehension could lose validity if it allows too little time to take the test. It might actually measure reading speed rather than reading comprehension.

Reliability

Reliability refers to the sameness of test results. For example, if you take a learning ability test today, the results should be similar to those you would receive if you took the test tomorrow or next month for the test to be considered reliable.

Practicality

Practicality involves the cost and convenience of a test. A standardized test must be practical within the setting where it is to be given. If the results are too difficult for school personnel to interpret in terms that will have application for your school experience, the test should probably not be administered. Also, if the test would have to be given to all the students in a school one-by-one, it may be too time consuming to be convenient. If the test will result in unreasonable cost to the student, again its practicality is in doubt.

Test Development

Developing a standardized test takes the work of many people and several years' time. Psychometrists must think of the nation as a classroom. The different abilities and needs of the thousands of students who take the tests must be considered.

Thorough Research

A good standardized test has carefully planned test items. As part of the planning, test makers gather information from many schools. This research forms the basis upon which final decisions are made about which items should appear.

Test makers must gauge what students at certain grade levels should be able to answer. Course goals and facts given in textbooks are considered. The ways the information is presented and the skills students need to work the material are important.

The length of the standardized test and its items will vary in appropriateness from level to level. By junior high, an increasing amount of specific knowledge is required to answer the items, and the tests become longer. The items are more detailed, and the language becomes more complex.

When norm groups are used in developing a test, if most students answer an item under consideration correctly, test makers will probably reject it. This is because the item does not help in comparing individual students. On a norm-referenced achievement test, for example, if students seem able to answer the question correctly whether they have received any instruction or not, the item is likely a poor measure of learning in the subject area.

For norm-referenced tests, test makers must also check whether an item is most often answered correctly by students with high overall scores. Sometimes the same learning is tested at several levels. If so, a check is made to see if the item is answered correctly more times as it appears in the upper levels of the test. Items showing this pattern are often used only at these levels and are eliminated from the lower levels.

The number of students answering correctly is not a factor in selecting items for a criterion-referenced achievement test. The important consideration for items on this type of test is that they measure something the students should know. Comparison of students is not a goal of the test. Measuring individual learning is.

Clear Directions

Directions to the student are carefully developed. They may be rewritten many times to be sure that everyone taking the test understands what is expected.

Directions are carefully checked to ensure the words are familiar to students at the age and grade level taking the test. Test makers must also see that directions are written clearly. This is important on standardized tests because a direction that is even slightly misunderstood may cause you to miss an item even when you know the answer.

Fair Items

Those who prepare standardized tests try to make them fair to all students who take them. Test takers may be from urban, suburban, and rural areas. If a test of learning ability or aptitude asks the students to identify machines, the selections should not include a milking machine and a tractor. The test maker knows that these machines might be recognized instantly by students who live in rural areas. But they might be completely unknown by students who have always lived in the city.

Makers of standardized tests try to make them fair to all students who take them.

Standardized tests may be given to students whose families have both large and small incomes. A reading comprehension item on an achievement test that asks a question about a new home computer or a sable coat is more likely to be answered correctly by a student whose family has a high income.

The test makers also watch for items that are answered correctly by almost everyone in one geographic region but not another. For example, a saguaro cactus may be identified readily by students who live in the Southwest. Spanish moss may be familiar to those from the South. Neither should probably appear in a standardized test item to be given all over the country.

The test makers must also be alert to the fact that some objects have different names in different parts of the country. For example, rubber bands are called gum bands in some parts of the country. On standardized tests, the term *rubber bands* should be used, since this is the most common term.

Appropriate Test Presentation

There is a wide range of standardized tests, and various materials may come with each kind. For example, student answer sheets and an examiner's manual are made available through many test publishing companies. The manual often provides background material telling about the development of the test and giving specific suggestions on how to present and administer it.

Great care must be taken by the test administrators to present the test according to the directions. Individual tests are often given by highly trained test administrators because the answers are evaluated as they are given. Presenting the test and evaluating the answer at the same time is not easy, and specialized training in just how to give the test is required.

But many standardized tests can be properly given by teachers and counselors at the schools. Since standardized tests should take place in conditions that are as uniform as possible, the test givers are provided with specific instructions on how this is to be done.

Often the instructions to the person giving the test include statements to be repeated word-for-word. Other instructions may include suggestions to check the condition of the room for lighting, comfortable temperature, clear desk space, and other physical factors. Sometimes directions to students are recorded on a cassette. Then the teacher is instructed to play the recording. All the students receive exactly the same directions in the same tone of voice, in the same speech pattern, and with the same emphasis.

Sufficient Answering Time

Another part of preparing a good standardized test is allowing the proper amount of time for you to answer the questions. Each test is to be completed in a set time, which is checked and adjusted as necessary during test development. Many standardized tests are planned so that you work for no more than two hours without a rest period.

Tests for individuals often take longer than tests for groups. Often all or part of an individual test is oral. The responses to oral items take longer than those for written ones.

In addition to controlling the overall time of the test, the sections that make it up are assigned times. When the section changes, test makers should allow you enough time to make the transition. For example, if you change from circling one of four answers to writing the letter of an answer in a box, you should have an adjustment period in between to refocus your attention.

Compilation of Research

Test preparation nears completion when all the results of research are in and comparisons are made. Teachers of students in the experimental groups may be asked to give their comments on the test items and make suggestions for improvement.

When the results have been studied, a final list of items is prepared. Then the standardized test is complete and ready for use.

Test Administration

Schedules

Most schools set aside a block of class time for giving standardized tests—rescheduling, shortening, or eliminating classes. When testing is completed, classes return to the normal schedule.

Some types of standardized tests are given more often than others. Since tests of achievement are so helpful in interpreting student progress, they are given most often. Learning ability, aptitude and interest, and personality tests are given less frequently, as are competency tests, which are not given at all in some schools.

Standardized tests are most frequently given in the fall or in the spring. That is, they are given either before students get into an established class pattern or as they are about to break pattern for a spring or summer vacation.

Locations

Standardized tests may be given in classrooms, study halls, school libraries, gymnasiums, auditoriums, and lunchrooms. In some cases, students might be tested in their homerooms. Often classes will take the test at the same time. Every effort is made to keep the test-taking situations as much alike as possible.

Test Items

You will encounter many different types of test questions, or items, on standardized tests. Each has its own answering strategies.

Some standardized tests, like personality tests, require no preparation. To prepare for competency and other standardized tests designed to measure knowledge, the best preparation is regular study and good health.

The rest of this section presents thirteen common standardized test items.

Reading Comprehension Items

Reading comprehension items are designed to test your ability to read and understand material that you are seeing for the first time. You need not know anything beforehand about the subject to be able to answer the questions correctly.

These items usually have two parts. The first is generally a short reading selection from an essay or story. Sometimes the reading selection is a poem. The second part contains one or more questions about the reading selection. Several choices will be given for your answer to each question.

Strategies

For many reading comprehension items, it may be worthwhile for you to scan the answers before you begin reading the selection. This approach allows you to focus on relevant information as you read the passage. Then read the passage carefully. Reread or at least rescan the passage in order to set your understanding.

Knowing the way ideas relate to one another is important for answering reading comprehension questions properly. Has one situation caused another? Is one idea part of another idea?

For reading comprehension items, scan the questions and answers before reading the selection.

You may have to be able to tell the difference between broad subjects and narrow subjects. For example, money is a broad subject. Coins is a narrower subject. Pennies is an even narrower subject. Pennies minted in 1981 is extremely narrow when compared to the subject of money. Sometimes your questions will include broad and narrow items like these for the topic, and you must be able to distinguish among them to answer correctly.

Reading comprehension questions may also ask you to find the likenesses and differences between two or more things. Or you may be asked to show the order in which events happen. Some questions may ask you to decide if one event is going to lead to another event.

In some questions, you may have to infer the answers, or read between the lines. This means that you will have to use reasoning to find the answer. You may be called upon to make a generalization.

Correctly reading the directions for reading comprehension items is crucial. Be careful if the question asks you to respond "based on the passage" or "according to the selection." These phrases mean that even though you may know one of the choices to be true, if the passage does not make any mention of the fact, you should look for another choice.

Be careful when directions for a reading comprehension item ask you to select the best answer from among several. When you see this type of direction, it means that more than one answer is right. You may also be asked to find the wrong answer to a question. Your choice then may be an answer that is too general or too specific or that gives insufficient information to answer the question correctly.

Verbal Analogy Items

A verbal analogy successfully mixes two pairs of dissimilar words creating a relationship between them. Verbal analogy items are designed to test your ability to see that relationship. They also test your vocabulary.

Usually an item will present three words and ask you to supply the missing fourth word. You will often be given three or four choices to complete the analogy. Look at the following set of words:

nose:person::beak:duck

This is a completed verbal analogy. It says, "a nose has the same relationship to a person that a beak has to a duck." If you were to see this verbal analogy on a standardized test, it might be written as follows:

Example:

nose:person::_____:duck
a. smell
b. beak
c. feathers

*Verbal analogy items
test your vocabulary
and your ability to see
relationships between
words.*

Strategies

The first thing to decide when answering a verbal analogy item is what the words in the given pair have to do with each other. In the example "nose:person," you might say that a person smells and breathes through the nose. Looking at the other side of the analogy, you could ask, "What does the duck use to smell and breathe?"

The item gives you three choices. The first choice, *a,* cannot be correct because the analogy is not asking what the nose does, but what a duck has that it uses the same way that a person uses a nose. And a duck does not use its feathers, *c,* to smell and breathe. The correct answer is *b.*

Example:

  cat:kitten::dog:puppy

You would read this verbal analogy as follows: "Cat has the same relationship to kitten as dog has to puppy." What does the (:) between cat and kitten do? It says that what follows is the name of this animal when it is young. In the completed verbal analogy, the double colon (::) tells you dog and puppy have the same relationship as cat and kitten, in that order. The same relationship applies to both pairs. Otherwise, the analogy is incorrect.

Think of a relationship that you can apply to two dissimilar words to create a verbal analogy. Consider *pin* and *house* for the two different words. For the relationship, try "give a larger version of this." A larger version of a pin might be a nail. A larger version of a house might be a mansion.

Example:

  pin:nail::house:mansion

Consider another example. This time use the relationship "usually goes with." For the two different words, try *bacon* and *jelly.* Something that usually goes with bacon is eggs. Something that usually goes with jelly is peanut butter.

Sometimes analogies are written so that the relationship works across the double colon. The examples given earlier might be rearranged like this:

If you come across a verbal analogy that has been arranged this way, you can change it mentally or on scratch paper so that the related words are together. You may be able to quickly solve a verbal analogy item in which the words seem to have no connection by using this strategy. Just be sure to keep the words in the proper order. That is, always switch the second word in the first pair with the first word in the second pair.

On some standardized tests, instead of completing a second pair of words from a list of choices, you are given one pair and asked to match it to a second finished pair, the words of which are linked by the same relationship.

Comma has the same relationship to *pause* as *period* has to *stop*. The relationship is "tell what this is used for." A comma is used in a sentence to tell the reader to pause. A period is used in a sentence to tell the reader to come to a full stop.

Another type of verbal analogy that you may find on tests requires that you fill in a word on both sides of the double colon. In the following example, another difference is that the verbal analogy uses a complete sentence form instead of colons to organize the item.

Example:

Fill in the blanks with the pair of words that makes the sentence true or sensible.

_____ is to night as breakfast is to _____

a. supper/dinette   d. morning/supper
b. gentle/morning   e. flow/enjoy
c. door/corner

You may find this type of question more difficult because there is no complete pair given for you to consider. Remember that the same relationship must operate between both pairs of words in the completed analogy. If you chose *a*, there would be one relationship between the first pair of words (supper is to night) and a different relationship between the second pair of words (breakfast is to dinette). The only relationship that works using the choices offered is "when this meal is usually served."

Remember that the authors of standardized tests try to write questions that everyone will be able to understand. Even if you like to eat supper at night and breakfast at the dinette, most people would agree with the analogy created by choice *d*.

Many students sometimes give incorrect answers for analogy questions because they choose word pairs that seem correct but actually show opposite relationships.

Example:

river:creek::
a. street:alley   d. pond:lake
b. hill:tunnel   e. island: peninsula
c. path:sidewalk

The relationship between *river* and *creek* is one of relative size. A river is a larger version of a creek. Some students might select *d* as their answer because a lake is a larger version of a pond. This would be incorrect, however, because it changes the direction of the relationship. You must not reverse the order of the words in one pair if you wish to still have the same relationship apply to both pairs. It would be incorrect to answer "river is to creek as alley is to street." The correct answer to the example is *a*—river:creek::street:alley, "large is to small as large is to small," or, specifically, "river is to creek as street is to alley."

One clue to look for when working with analogy questions is similarities in the parts of speech of the words being used. Often, the first word in the first pair will be the same part of speech as the first word in the second pair. The second word in the first pair will be the same part of speech as the second word in the second pair. The analogy can be set up as follows:

Examples:

    a. noun:noun::noun:noun, or
       bacon:eggs::jelly:peanut butter
    b. verb:noun::verb:noun, or
       smell:nose::see:eye
    c. adverb:verb::adverb:verb, or
       quietly:study::loudly:play

Knowing the parts of speech can allow you to eliminate as possible answers any choices that do not follow the correct pattern. Review the parts of speech before taking any test that will have verbal analogy items.

As you prepare for verbal analogies, also become familiar with this list of relationships that they commonly show.

Relationship	Example
1. means the same as (equality)	tall:high
2. means the opposite of (opposition)	little:big
3. is a type of or an adjective describing (description)	Merino:sheep
4. is a part of	child:humanity

5. usually comes before or turns into (process)	tadpole:frog
6. is a cause/effect of	rain:flood
7. usually goes with (companionship)	bacon:eggs
8. is used by (uses)	saw:carpenter
9. is made from or made of (manufacture)	cloth:cotton
10. is a larger/smaller version of	river:creek
11. is more/less than (intensity)	torture:irritate
12. takes place before/after (order)	morning:noon
13. is a measure of	inch:distance
14. has the purpose of	food:nutrition
15. originated in	chicken:egg
16. is located in	Paris:France

Properly reading directions for verbal analogy items is of great importance.

Properly reading directions for answering verbal analogy questions is of great importance. The form may be quite different from test to test, and directions may change within sections of the same test. Be sure you understand how you are to figure and mark answers before you begin.

It is a good idea to check the number of your answer against the number of the question often as you mark your answers. Losing your place and skipping a question is easy to do when answering verbal analogy items.

Number Series Items

Number series items are in many ways like verbal analogy items. Both are designed to test your ability to recognize a relationship that is being applied. The difference is that instead of working with two pairs of words, you work with a series of numbers and select another number that coordinates with the series.

Strategies

When you look at the numbers in a series, first try to see what is happening to each as you read from left to right. Are the numbers getting larger? Are they getting smaller? Are they getting larger, then smaller, and so on? Look at the following number series:

Example:

21   18   15   12   9   _____

You will notice as you read from left to right that the numbers are becoming smaller. This is a clue that the way to find the answer may be to subtract a number from each number in the series. It is rather easy to see that the relationship in this case is "subtract 3." You know that the number 6 belongs in the blank because it is the result of 9 minus 3. Now try a more complicated series:

Example:

10   11   13   16   20   25   _____

You will see right away that the same number is not being added each time, though it is clear that the relationship for every number involves addition, since the numbers are increasing. To answer this problem, you should find which numbers are being added each time to see if you can discover a pattern:

10   11   13   16   20   25   _____
   + 1   + 2   + 3   + 4   + 5

You can see that the relationship here is to add counting numbers, starting with 1, to each number in the series. The next counting number in the series is 6. Adding 6 to 25, you get 31. The completed series will be 10, 11, 13, 16, 20, 25, 31.

Sometimes finding out how much has been added to or subtracted from a number in the series will not, by itself, let you discover what the relationship is for the number series. Look at the item below:

Example:

1   6   36   216   _____

In this example, 5 has been added to the first number, 30 to the second, and 180 to the third. There seems at first to be no pattern to the series. You will have to think of it in another way. You know that adding 5 to 1 will give you 6, but another way to get from 1 to 6 is to multiply 6 times 1. Now try "multiply times 6" as the relationship.

$$1 \times 6 = 6$$
$$6 \times 6 = 36$$
$$36 \times 6 = 216$$

The relationship for this number series is to multiply the number times 6, beginning with 1. The next number in the series is 1,296.

In all the examples given so far, each number in the series followed a pattern of becoming larger or smaller. This is not always the case. Look at the following number series:

Example:

    10 33 32 13 31 30 16 29 _____ _____

It is clear that some numerals are being added to and some are being subtracted from. Yet, you probably cannot see any pattern right away.

    10   33   32   13
      $+22$ -1 -19 $+18$
    31   30   16   29 _____ _____
      -1 -14 $+13$

You will have to try a different strategy. First, find any numbers appearing in the series that seem to go together. You can see right away that 33, 32, 31, 30, and 29 are in order by the relationship "subtract 1." The remaining numbers in the series, 10, 13, and 16, are in order by the relationship "add 3." If you split the number series into two parts, you see how the pattern works.

    10   13   16   _____
     33 32   31 30   29   _____

Each number in the top line has had 3 added to it. Each number in the lower line has had 1 subtracted from it. The next number in the lower line is 28. The next number in the top line is 19. The completed series will be: 10, 33, 32, 13, 31, 30, 16, 29, 28, 19.

The numbers can be odd or even, prime numbers, or square roots:

$$2 \quad -1 \quad 6 \quad -4 \quad 10 \quad -16 \quad 14 \ \_\_\_\_$$

Split this number series into negative numbers and positive numbers:

$$2 \quad\quad 6 \quad\quad 10 \quad\quad\quad 14 \ \_\_\_\_$$
$$-1 \quad -4 \quad\ -16$$

You can see right away that the relationship on the top line is to add 4 to each number. You can also determine that the same number is not being added to each number in the lower line. Multiplication or division may be involved instead. Since the absolute value, or distance from zero, of the numbers is increasing, the relationship must be multiplication by some number. In this case, the relationship is to multiply by 4.

$$-1 \ \times \ 4 \ = \ -4$$
$$-4 \ \times \ 4 \ = \ -16$$
$$-16 \times \ 4 \ = \ -64$$

The correctly completed series is therefore:

$$2 \quad\quad -1 \quad\quad 6 \quad\quad -4 \quad\quad 10 \quad\quad -16 \quad\quad 14 \quad\quad \underline{-64}$$

You have seen some number series questions that are relatively difficult and relatively easy to answer. Never make the easy ones harder than they really are. Look at the series of fractions below:

Example:

$$\tfrac{1}{2} \quad\quad \tfrac{1}{3} \quad\quad \tfrac{1}{4} \quad\quad \tfrac{1}{5} \quad\quad \_\_\_\_$$

To find the answer, all you have to recognize is that the denominator is being increased by 1 for each fraction in the series. Even if you did not know how to use fractions, you could probably choose $\tfrac{1}{6}$ as the answer for this series.

Number series questions sometimes ask you to point out a number in the series that is out of place. It is important that you read the directions carefully when answering this type of question.

Example:

Which number in the following series is wrong?

1 8 2 8 3 8 4 8 5 8 7 8 (   )

Most students will notice right away that every other number in the series is 8 and will mentally split the series into two parts:

1		2		3		4		5		7	
	8		8		8		8		8		8

Among the counting numbers in the top row, 7 is out of place because 6 is missing. Therefore, the number 7 is the answer because the directions ask you to supply the incorrect number in the series.

We have been solving number series so far by "filling in the blank." To answer questions on a standardized test, you usually find answers offered as choices *a, b, c, d,* or other appropriate identification labels. You will mark the correct space—ⓐ, ⓑ, ⓒ, ⓓ—on your answer sheet. There will be only one correct answer shown as a choice.

Do not be alarmed and give up if your first answer does not fit any of the choices. You may be using the wrong relationship to complete the number series. Think again and see if you can find another relationship that may apply. If you cannot do so right away, skip the item and go back to it later. Make sure also to skip the answer blank on the answer sheet.

Configuration series items test your ability to understand relationships.

Configuration Series Items

Like verbal analogy and number series items, configuration series items are designed to test your ability to understand relationships. A configuration is an arrangement of parts, such as in a figure. In configuration series items, two-dimensional figures change in some logical way. They may change in size, shape, color, or in content.

Usually configuration series items will show you three or four figures that are in order and will give you a choice of three or four figures to be the next in the series.

Only one of the choices is correct. You must determine which one it is.

Strategies

The figures in a configuration series will always appear in order from left to right. The choices will be labeled with numbers or letters. The same logic will always apply to every figure in the series. The choices of figures to be selected as answers will appear to the right of the series. Study this configuration problem:

Example:

Which figure is next in the series?

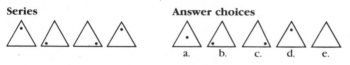

What is happening in each triangle in the series? The dot is moving from corner to corner in a counterclockwise fashion. It goes from top to lower left to lower right to top. Since the same rule that applies to the first four figures applies to the correct answer figure, answer *b* must be correct because that triangle shows the dot in the lower left corner. In this example, only one relationship is being applied to the figures. The dot is moving from corner to corner in a counterclockwise fashion.

More difficult problems will involve two or more relationships that are being applied at the same time. Two changes are happening in these figures:

Example:

Which figure is next in the series?

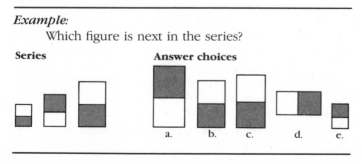

First, notice that the rectangles in the series alternate shading. The second change is that each rectangle is larger than the preceding one.

Before you look at the answer choices, you should try to form a picture of what the next configuration in the series is going to be. This way, you will avoid confusion. Since the last rectangle in the series is light over dark, you can guess that the answer rectangle should be dark over light. The answer rectangle should be a little bit larger than the last rectangle in the series. Only choice *a* is both dark over light and larger than the last figure.

Sometimes, new parts will be added to a configuration series as the figures progress from left to right. In the next example, the first figure contains a single symbol: a star. In every figure that follows, a new symbol is added, until the fourth figure contains four symbols: a star, a circle, a plus sign, and a dollar sign.

Because configuration series are visual, they can be deceptive.

Example:

Which figure is next in the series?

Series

*	O *	+ O	$ +
			* * O

Answer choices

* O *		$	× *
$		O	O
+ $		+	$ +
a.	b.	c.	d.

Just by discovering this rule, you can eliminate choices *b* and *c*, which have fewer parts than the fourth figure in the series.

What else is going on in the series? In every new figure, each symbol is in a different position. From figure 3 to figure 4, the + has moved from the upper left corner to the upper right corner, the ○ has moved from the upper right corner to the lower right corner, and the * has moved from the lower right corner to the lower left corner. Look at choice *a* in the answer set. There are three things wrong with this choice. First, the * is in the same position as in figure 1 of the series. Second, the ○ is in the same position as in figure 3. Third, instead of a new symbol being added to the set, only another $ has been added. Of the choices given, only *d* is correct. The position of every symbol in the figure has changed, and a new symbol, ×, has been added.

Remember that whenever you have to make a choice where two or more answers seem correct, you should always select the answer that best continues the configuration series in the same way that it has been progressing. In the example above, some students might have chosen *b* because they thought the series was going to start over again. Some students might have chosen *c* because they thought the series was going to decrease after reaching four parts. There is nothing, however, in the series to indicate that its pattern will either repeat or decrease.

Because configuration series are visual, they can be deceptive. You should always read the instructions carefully rather than interpreting the answers from the figures alone. As on all test items, careful reading of the directions is a must with configuration series questions.

Spatial Comprehension Items

Spatial comprehension items require that you mentally picture some real object in a variety of positions, that you assemble a real object in your mind, or that you visualize objects in space and move them to different positions. To work on these items, you must use your thinking skills and your imagination.

Usually these items will show a figure to the left. Then, a series of illustrations will appear to the right. They are the answer choices. You select the correct illustration according to what the directions call for.

Strategies

Read directions for items related to spatial comprehension with care. You must have a clear understanding of the exact shift in position asked for if you are to arrive at the right answer.

You will want to consider whether the movement described is in one direction or whether several levels of movement are described. It may be helpful to read the directions several times and work with an object (pen or pencil, for example) to make sure you understand each move. Ask yourself questions like these as you work spatial comprehension items:

1. Do you have the shape and size of the object clearly in mind?

2. Are you sure of the shape of each side of the object?

3. Are you able to picture yourself in one spot and the object in motion?

4. Can you picture the object from each side?

5. Are the straight edges of the object level or slanted?

6. Is the object moving in more than one direction?

Writing Items

Writing items are designed to test your ability in capitalization, punctuation, grammar, usage, and organization of ideas. Some of these tests also ask you to do an essay. The principles of essay writing are basically the same for standardized test items as for teachers' test items, which are discussed in Section III. Review the essay portion of that section if you are about to take a standardized test that will include an essay.

This portion describes objective-type writing items that appear on standardized tests. Tests group the items under varied subheadings, such as language mechanics or language expression.

Strategies

For writing items, you most often indicate the incorrect use of a symbol or word or choose, from a multiple-choice selection, the symbol or word needed to complete a sentence. The directions for writing items vary, so read them and the entire item with care. Here are some examples:

Punctuation:

Choose the correct punctuation mark to end the following sentence:

What time did the students leave school
a. (.)   b. (,)   c. (?)√   d. (!)

Grammar:

Find the correct word to complete the following sentence:

Max ran the race as fast as _____ could.
a. they   b. she   c. he√   d. me

Usage:

Find the incorrect underlined word or words:

While running the race, the boy ran out of energy
     a   b
and must slow down so that he could finish racing.
  c√   d

Organizing ideas:

1. Select the answer that shows the best order for these sentences:
   a. She bought her ticket at the door.
   b. She parked the car in the parking lot.
   c. Then she went to the refreshment stand.
   d. Julietta drove to the movies.
      1. c-a-b-d 2. d-b-a-c√ 3. b-a-d-c 4. a-d-c-b

2. Choose the pair of sentences that best develops the topic sentence:

   A visit to the Southwest in the spring is fascinating for newcomers.
   a. The land is bleak and the temperature unbearably hot. Flooding occurs frequently in areas that monsoons hit in July and August.
   b. The verbena bloom early, laying a multicolored carpet across the valleys. When the snow melts in the mountains, the gullies in the lowlands swell into refreshing creeks.√

    c. The traffic is lighter in the Southwest than in more densely populated areas of the United States. But you may see many more campers on the road.

3. Choose the best concluding sentence for the following paragraph:

The shift to industry helped make Rhode Island one of the nation's most urban states. There are only eight cities in all of Rhode Island.
    a. But about 85 per cent of the state's citizens live in urban areas.√
    b. Newport's Touro Synagogue is the nation's oldest existing synagogue.
    c. The textile industry eventually declined in importance.

A number of thinking operations will usually be needed to make the correct selection in writing items.

Example:

Which underlined word or words should be changed?

The newspaper <u>reported</u> that 12 people
                       a

<u>were selected</u> for the jury, but the judge <u>will not</u>
       b   c

open the trial for several days because the defense attorney <u>was involved</u> in another case.
               d

You must read through the paragraph and determine the relationship of events before selecting an answer. As you check the underlined verbs in the above paragraph, you should realize that most of the paragraph is in the past tense. Only one underlined verb is in the future tense. After reading the paragraph carefully, you should become aware that the paragraph reads more clearly if <u>will not</u> is changed to <u>would not</u>. Thus, <u>will not</u> is incorrect, and *c* is the answer.

If there is an item you are unsure of, you may find it useful mentally to repeat the sentence or sentences that make it up. Do so for each answer choice. Chances are the correct answer will come to you because you have reviewed how you would say the sentence. Be careful with this technique, however; many of the words and rules appearing on your standardized test are chosen because they are frequently misused by many people.

Vocabulary Items

Vocabulary items are designed to test your knowledge and understanding of words. These skills are also important for other standardized test items.

Strategies

Vocabulary items can take several forms.

Examples:

    A. Choose the synonym for the underlined word.
       <u>illuminate</u>
       a. sick   c. darken
       b. minute   d. lighten√

    B. Choose the antonym for the underlined word.
       <u>reproach</u>
       a. commend√ b. require c. request d. blame

Among the choices, a vocabulary item will probably include both an antonym and a synonym for the underlined word (darken/lighten; commend/blame). If you can find a pair of opposites among the choices, one is probably the correct answer.

Vocabulary items can also give you a sentence that has a word missing. You are shown several words and must choose one to complete the sentence so that it will make sense.

Example:

Choose the word that will make the best, truest, and most sensible sentence.

There is no man so _____ that something good cannot be found in him.
a. likable   b. bored   c. upright   d. wicked

This type of question requires you to do two things. You must understand the meaning of the sentence as a whole, and you must also understand its individual words. You should read the sentence and then try to find a word among the choices that means the opposite of *good.* *Wicked, d,* is the only appropriate choice among the words offered. Notice that *likable* and *upright* are both adjectives associated with "good."

Anticipate the correct answer before you see what the choices are.

When possible, anticipate the correct answer before you see what the choices are. Often, this will help you avoid becoming confused.

Example:

Induce means to
a. lead on   c. stymie
b. enroll   d. obtain unlawfully

Some careless students will choose *b, enroll,* which is the definition of *induct.* This choice will not tempt you if you have thought out the definition of *induce* before looking at the choices.

Sometimes, you can guess the meaning of an unfamiliar word by examining its parts. This is where knowledge of prefixes, suffixes, and root words comes in handy. Find a list of these in your dictionary and study them.

Example:

Choose the correct definition for the underlined word in the sentence.

Being a bibliophile helped Timmy enjoy his literature class.
a. dedicated scholar   b. successful athlete

---

c. lover of books√   d. confirmed dreamer
Bibl is the root word for "book."

Avoid quick decisions on vocabulary items.

Example:
    A <u>tenet</u> is
    a. a principle held as true   c. a renter
    b. a group of ten

Many students might choose *c, a renter,* for the correct answer here, confusing *tenet* with *tenant.* Others might choose *b, a group of ten,* seeing the syllable *ten* in *tenet.* The correct answer, however, is *a, a principle held as true.*

    Sometimes you may come across a word that you have seen but cannot define exactly.

Example:
    <u>Terminal</u> means the same as
    a. concluding   c. living in trees
    b. lengthy

Try to put the word into a phrase, such as "terminal illness." A terminal illness would lead to the conclusion of someone's life. Answer *a* is correct.

Spelling Items

Spelling items are designed to test your memory and understanding of basic rules of letter arrangement. Many intelligent students have difficulties with this skill. But there are ways to overcome them for the test.

Strategies

Standardized test writers use commonly misspelled words over and over in spelling items. Ask your teacher for a list of words commonly misspelled at or around your grade level. Practice them with a partner, if possible. Ask your teacher where you can find a list of spelling rules. Learn them. Keep up with your spelling lessons at school. Make

Standardized test writers use commonly misspelled words in spelling items.

lists of words you misspell often. Review them before the test.

Sometimes we misspell words because we mispronounce them. Sound out words—even exaggerate them. Say *"bus-i-ness"* rather than *"bisness,"* for example. During the test, sound out the words mentally. Ask your teacher where you can find a list of commonly mispronounced words and study them.

Spelling items vary. They sometimes ask you to find a misspelling among a group of correctly spelled words. Or they could ask you to find a correct word in a group of misspellings. Make sure you know what you are looking for before you answer any items.

If you don't know an answer, narrow the field. As appropriate, eliminate words you know are correct or misspelled. Then see if you can make a choice from what is left.

When spelling tests are oral, concentrate. Sometimes the test giver will read a word for you that you will write down or whose correct spelling you will select from choices on an answer sheet. Listen carefully to the word as the test giver pronounces it. Sound it out to yourself. Then write or choose the answer.

Mathematics Items

Mathematics items are designed to test your computational skills and your mathematical reasoning. You may have to use several mathematics operations to arrive at a solution. For some mathematics items, however, you should do no computation at all. These items simply require common sense based on your knowledge of mathematics concepts.

Find out if you can bring scratch paper and calculators to your mathematics test.

There are two general types of mathematics items that you will encounter on standardized tests. The first type mainly involves routine computations. These problems are relatively straightforward: you are asked, for example, to do mathematical operations such as add, subtract, multiply, or divide numbers. The second type of item requires you to solve problems presented in words. You usually have to compute to solve word problems, also. This portion will deal mainly with word problems.

Strategies

Before any mathematics test, find out if you can bring scratch paper, calculators, and other aids to the test. If you can, bring and use them.

Here are eight steps that you should always follow if you are preparing to take a test with word problems. Some of these also apply to computation problems.

1. If you may solve the problems in any order, do the easy ones first and then work up to the most difficult.

2. Make sure you know what the problem is asking before you begin.

3. If you can guess the answer without doing any calculations, do so.

4. If you cannot guess an answer, organize the information given. Disregard irrelevant information.

5. Estimate your answer before doing any calculations.

6. When you have finished the problem, compare your answer with your estimate to see if your answer is reasonable.

7. Double-check the word problem to make sure you have the answer the problem was asking for.

8. Check your answer to see if it is practical.

Keep in mind that mathematical reasoning does not always involve numbers, but only your mastery of a concept, such as the concept of quantity.

Example:
> Bob, Dino, and Scott entered a pie-eating contest.
> Dino ate more pie than Scott but less than Bob.
> Who ate the smallest amount of pie?
> a. Bob   b. Scott√   c. Dino   d. Dino and Scott

There were no numbers needed to write or answer this item.

The following is a long problem. Irrelevant information for this and the rest of the examples in this portion are shown in parentheses.

Example:

Min, Josh, Meg, and Julio (like hamburgers. They want to) keep track of the amount they will spend on hamburgers (during a trip). Min (stops) twice a day for one hamburger at 60 cents each. Josh (stops) four times a day for one hamburger at 55 cents each. Meg stops once a day for one hamburger at 75 cents. Julio stops twice a day for two hamburgers at 50 cents each. (It takes) Meg and Julio three days (to make the trip and) Min and Josh four days. What amount will they pay for all the hamburgers?
a. $1,845   b. $21.85√   c. $24.60   d. $18.85

To solve this item, all you need to know is how to multiply and add with decimals. Start by eliminating choice *a* as unreasonable. The answer is probably *b* or *d*, which both end in 85 cents. Now organize your information in a chart like the one shown below. First multiply to find out how much each person spent on hamburgers. Then add these amounts together to find the answer.

	Cost	×	No. per day	×	No. of days	=	Subtotal
Min	$.60	×	2	×	4	=	$4.80
Josh	.55	×	4	×	4	=	8.80
Meg	.75	×	1	×	3	=	2.25
Julio	.50	×	4	×	3	=	+ 6.00
		Total cost of hamburgers for entire trip				=	$21.85

Computation problems look easier than word problems to many people.

Example:

$$\begin{array}{r} 250 \\ 2\overline{)500} \end{array}$$

If you translate word problems into computation problems, you will be able to reason out the answers more easily. Sometimes you can reduce problems to a simple computational form and do all the figuring in your head.

Example:

> (Gary is traveling on an airplane flying at) 500 miles an hour. (Gary travels for) 30 minutes. How far has Gary flown?

Your problem here is the same as in the computation example above. The same mathematical concept, division of whole numbers, is involved. The answer, 250, should be just as quickly arrived at because you know 30 minutes is one-half hour ($\frac{500}{2} = 250$).

Perhaps you have been adding and subtracting mixed fractions in class.

Examples:

> a. $3\frac{3}{4} + 2\frac{7}{8} + 4\frac{1}{2} + 3\frac{3}{4} = 14\frac{7}{8}$
> b. $4\frac{1}{2} + 6\frac{1}{2} + 5\frac{1}{2} + 3\frac{1}{2} + 10 = 30$
> c. $50 - 44\frac{7}{8} = 5\frac{1}{8}$

Here is a word problem using the same computations:

Example:

> (Sally Smith bought) 50 pounds (of chicken on sale and put it in her freezer. She let her family and friends come get chicken whenever they wished. They weighed it on a scale near the freezer and noted how much they took. At the end of the week, Sally found the following notes:)

Fran $3\frac{3}{4}$ lb	Tom $4\frac{1}{2}$ lb
Jack $2\frac{7}{8}$ lb	Jill $6\frac{1}{2}$ lb
Mary $4\frac{1}{2}$ lb	Bert $5\frac{1}{2}$ lb

Dick $3\frac{3}{4}$ lb Amy $3\frac{1}{2}$ lb

Juanita 10 lb

How many pounds (did Sally have) left (at the end of the week)?

a. 61.8 lb b. $5\frac{1}{8}$ lb✓ c. $6\frac{3}{8}$ lb d. $6\frac{1}{2}$ lb

Eliminate answer a as unreasonable. Then, by adding the total taken and subtracting it from 50, you find the answer, b. To simplify this process, you might first split the mixed fractions into two convenient groups for addition: ($3\frac{3}{4}$ + $2\frac{7}{8}$ + $4\frac{1}{2}$ + $3\frac{3}{4}$ = $14\frac{7}{8}$) and ($4\frac{1}{2}$ + $6\frac{1}{2}$ + $5\frac{1}{2}$ + $3\frac{1}{2}$ + 10 = 30). Then add the sum of those operations ($14\frac{7}{8}$ + 30 = $44\frac{7}{8}$). Finally, subtract the last sum from 50 (50 − $44\frac{7}{8}$ = the answer, $5\frac{1}{8}$).

Speed-Test Items

Speed-test items are designed to show that you can perform tasks accurately and rapidly. The items are often used to measure clerical skills such as filing, checking for errors, and counting. Speed-test items may also be used to measure performance on office machines such as the typewriter or word processor. There are other timed items where you are asked to skim or scan a passage and select an answer.

Strategies

In reading directions for speed tests, note how much time you are given to work on the test. It may be split into different sections. When you reach the end of a section, relax. You will probably be instructed to go no farther until told to do so.

Be sure that you understand how you will be given the signal to go on to the next section. Sometimes verbal instructions are given. In other test situations, a bell or buzzer will signal the beginning of work on a section.

You do not always have to read all the choices shown in speed-test items. When you find an answer you know is correct, mark it and go to the next problem. For example, if you are asked to consider four lists of items and find the one arranged in alphabetical order, if the first list is alphabetical, do not read the other lists. If you do, you will waste your time.

If a correction-for-guessing formula is used to score your speed test, you probably should not guess on the speed-test items, since guessing may lower your score. Otherwise, when the time draws short, you may want to mark as many answers as possible, even if you have not read the items left.

Attitude Items

Attitude items are designed to test how you feel and think about yourself and how you relate to others. They may ask you to identify your thoughts about your family and acquaintances. To score accurately, you must be honest in your response. That is the best strategy for an attitude-item test.

Answers to attitude items are sometimes simply yes or no. For others, you may be asked to circle SA for strongly agree, A for agree, D for disagree, or SD for strongly disagree.

Often, these items provide statements that present the same subject in both positive and negative forms. Generally, these forms are not together but are scattered throughout the test.

Examples:

Answer the statements yes or no:

I like myself.
I expect little success at school.
Life will improve greatly in the years ahead.
I do not like myself.
What happens to me depends on me.

When reading directions, you will want to check the way you are to show your answers. Attitude items often have few answers to choose from, so you will want to be sure you understand the answer system. Since attitude items are often developed to ask the same question in different ways, you should also concentrate on how the questions are phrased. You do not want to misrepresent your feelings because you misread a choice.

Here are some attitude items for you to review. How would you respond to these statements?

A.	I enjoy most of my classes at school.		YES	NO	
	Most of my instructors are good teachers.		YES	NO	
	The subjects I study interest me.		YES	NO	
	I am my own best friend.		YES	NO	
B.	The best years are ahead.	SA	A	D	SD
	I will be a success at the work I choose.	SA	A	D	SD
	I will be happy with the work I choose.	SA	A	D	SD

Listening Items

Some tests have listening items that require you to listen to a sentence, words, or a whole story read by the test giver or played on a recorder. These types of items are given to individuals or groups. An answer sheet or booklet gives you choices you pick from to fill in missing words or to answer questions in response to what you hear. You must listen carefully to figure out the correct answers.

The skills that listening tests are designed to measure vary from test to test but can include recognizing words and phrases; identifying problems; understanding words and ideas; identifying main ideas; associating details; understanding purpose; and drawing conclusions.

Strategies

Directions for listening items will generally tell you how answers are to be indicated and about the organization of the test. Often, you listen to a paragraph or sentence and then fill in missing words on the answer sheet.

Sometimes the answers to choose from are listed in multiple-choice form. If you are listening to a cassette, you may be told to stop it while you write or mark your answer. Make sure in any case that you know how to operate the recorder before you begin. Of course, you should test the cassette recorder to make sure it works before the test starts.

In the following example, you would listen to the sentence and then mark your answer on an answer sheet:

Example:

The test giver reads, "On the day of the big race, Joe ran the fastest." Your answer sheet reads:

Joe _____ the race.
a. ran in   b. won√   c. lost   d. missed

Here, you check the correct answer, b.

Never allow yourself to become distracted during a test of your listening skills. If there are any unusual distractions, such as noise or activity going on around you, tell the test giver. But if the distractions are minor, you are expected to be able to ignore them. That is a part of good listening.

One of the reasons listening skills tests are recorded is that the test makers want all students to have the same opportunity to hear and understand the items. If you are having trouble hearing your test, you are at a disadvantage. Make sure to ask to be moved to a better location.

Never allow yourself to become distracted during a test of your listening skills.

Speaking Items

Speaking items are designed to test your speaking skills. These items are not used so often as tests where answers are written.

Tests requiring short spoken answers are given individually and can be quite time-consuming. But they can be used to meet students' special needs. For example, a student who has recently come from another country where another language is spoken may be able to speak but not read or write in the test language.

Some standardized tests given at the secondary school level measure your ability to speak publicly; that is, to communicate with an audience. Often, you will have to persuade someone that your viewpoint is correct. You have to develop arguments that support your viewpoint. One or two evaluators measure your skills in speaking using a scale that lists different aspects of your speech like organization and strength of argument. Each aspect can be rated as inadequate, minimal, adequate, or superior.

Strategies

When directions for giving short answers in speaking items are read aloud, listen carefully. Ask questions about any parts of the directions that are unclear. Sometimes directions for speaking items change as the test goes on. Be alert for these changes. Remain calm, and speak up when giving your answer.

If you are to speak publicly, you may have time limitations. When organizing your thoughts for a speech, consider your time restrictions. Be sure you cover all the major points of your argument. Make each point simple and clear when you present it. Cover a few major points rather than many small ones.

Test Terms

ability grading Using a student's demonstrated level of achievement to set that student's expected level of achievement.

accountability The reporting, such as to communities, of the educational progress students are making.

achievement test A test that measures how much you have learned and what skills you have acquired.

alternate-response item An objective-test item that offers a choice of two or more answers, such as true or false or yes or no.

aptitude and interest test A test given to a person to find out for what work, studies, or skills that person is best suited.

battery A series of tests that covers the subjects you study in school. An achievement test generally consists of a battery of tests.

bell curve Also called a *normal curve;* a graphical arrangement of scores from lowest to highest to form a bell-shaped curve. The lowest and the highest scores occur with equal frequency; the score in the middle occurs most frequently.

calculated curve A curve that a teacher modifies when a class yields scores that will not fit into a normal, or bell, curve.

competency test An achievement test that measures your knowledge and ability in certain subjects or skills. Often you need to achieve a minimum score on a competency test to move on to the next learning level or to graduate from high school.

configuration series item A test item that consists of figures that change, for example, in size, shape, color, or content according to a logical rule.

correction-for-guessing A method of grading tests by which a teacher not only will add together the points for right answers, but will use a formula to take off points for wrong answers as well. So the more wrong answers you have due to guessing, the lower your score.

criterion-referenced test A test that measures how well you have learned what you have been taught in your classes by comparing your performance on the test to a specific set of learning objectives.

culturally biased test A test is culturally biased when students are unfamiliar with the terms or concepts used in the test because they are not common in the students' cultures.

diagnostic test A test that helps you find out why you repeat mistakes or have other learning difficulties.

essay test A test made up of a question or questions that ask you to explain, discuss, summarize, outline, or examine a topic by writing in a sensible, organized fashion.

evaluation The way in which your teacher finds out how well you are doing in your studies. The results of a test you take is one way of evaluating your progress.

extended-response item A type of essay question that allows you to express not only what you know but also your opinions.

fill-in test An objective test made up of incomplete sentences where you must fill in the missing information.

fixed standard A predetermined set of achievement expectations that are based on course goals. Grades are determined by comparing each student's performance with the fixed standard.

free-response test A test that is made up of items in which you supply the answer, such as fill-in, short-answer, oral, and essay items.

grade A means of evaluating your test performance where a letter or number is assigned to your score. An *A* is a superior grade, for example.

grading on a curve A method of grading in which students' scores are arranged from lowest to highest to form a curve such as a bell curve. Lines are then drawn so that specified percentages of students receive particular grades, such as high grades or low grades. A student's grade is determined by where his or her score falls on the curve.

group standard A group standard represents the achievement of a whole group of students on a norm-referenced test. Grades are determined by comparing each student's performance with the group.

group tests Tests that can be given to you and a number of other people at the same time by one examiner. These can be nonstandardized or standardized.

individual tests Tests that are given to only one person at a time. You can be given an individual test that is either nonstandardized or standardized. Many individual tests are voluntary.

instruction tests Most instruction tests, from weekly quizzes to the final, are teacher-designed tests. They not only measure achievement but are also useful as instruction and review aids.

intelligence test A standardized test that measures your general learning ability. The score is sometimes shown as an intelligence quotient (IQ).

interest inventory A check list that you complete, usually on an aptitude test, that asks questions about your interests and talents.

interest test See *aptitude and interest test*.

learning ability test A test that measures the knowledge and skills you have acquired as well as how well you use these skills; see also *intelligence test*.

mastery test A test that determines when you know a subject well enough to go on to the next level of learning in that subject.

matching test An objective test that features a subject column and a response column and requires you to match the information in each.

mathematics word items Word items used on mathematics tests to measure how well you understand and can apply the mathematics principles you have learned. The problems are presented in sentence form, with a question asked at the end.

multiple-choice test An objective test made up of individual questions that offer three or more answers to choose from.

nongraded A method of evaluation by which a grade is not assigned to classroom performance, including tests.

Students are evaluated in student-teacher and teacher-parent conferences. This method is said to de-emphasize competition for grades.

nonobjective test A test, like an art test, that a teacher scores by personal evaluation rather than by a fixed standard. Different forms of answers may be requested or acceptable.

nonstandardized test A test, usually teacher made or teacher selected, that evaluates your progress as one of a specific group of students in a particular subject area.

nonverbal test A test using, for example, pictures, symbols, or nonsense syllables that are equally unfamiliar to everyone taking the test.

norm A norm is an average score that is achieved on a test by a sample, or norm, group.

norm group A group of individuals that is as representative as possible of all students who are to take a test. See *norm*.

normal curve See *bell curve*.

norm-referenced test A test that compares your test results with those of a norm group rather than a fixed standard in order to determine your score.

number series item An item that requires you, after working with a series of numbers, to find the appropriate rule and apply it to find another number that coordinates with the series. The next number to appear in the series *5, 10, 15, 20* is *25*.

objective test A test that requires specific, short answers. True-false and multiple-choice questions are on objective-type tests.

open-book test A test that allows you to find the answer to the question or questions by using reference materials, books, or notes. Open-book tests can often be completed at home or in the library.

oral test A test that measures your ability to express your ideas or knowledge aloud.

oral comprehension test A test that measures your ability to listen to and understand what you hear.

percentile rank A ranking of scores by percentages.

performance test A test where you physically show what you know and whether you can perform a task skillfully and, in some cases, safely.

personality inventory A complex form of personality test that is given in later grades.

personality profile The scores from a personality test that are put together to form an overall picture of the test taker.

personality test A test that helps you identify how you feel about yourself and others.

practicality A standard for measuring whether a test's format and the time required for a test merit using it in a given educational setting.

pretest A test taken before any instruction begins to determine the level of knowledge and skills students possess. Pretests are usually tests for placement only.

psychometrists Scientists who are testing experts and who design standardized tests.

quality scale A scale that ranks samples of products from best to worst. Your teacher may compare your work to this type of scale in a performance test.

raw scores A tally of the exact number of items you answer correctly on a test.

readiness test A test that measures a child's ability to demonstrate mastery of the skills needed to begin formal instructional programs, such as in reading and mathematics.

reading comprehension test A test that measures your ability to read and understand material that you are seeing for the first time.

reliability A standard for determining the extent to which a test dependably or consistently measures the same thing every time it is used.

restricted-response item An essay item that limits your response in, for example, length, topic, or time.

sample group See *norm group.*

score The number of points earned in a test.

short-answer test An objective test that asks questions requiring brief answers; sometimes a one-word answer.

simulator A duplicate of a given set of conditions so that a student's performance can be evaluated within those conditions. For example, a road test in a traffic facility simulates actual road conditions.

spatial (space) comprehension test A test measuring whether you can imagine how three-dimensional objects will look fully assembled or in different positions.

specification list A teacher's list of what you should be able to accomplish to succeed on a performance, competency-based, or mastery test.

standard error of measurement An index that reflects the average of the difference between the students' scores as measured on a test and the students' true abilities. These abilities cannot be measured because perfect tests cannot be designed. Small standard errors of measurement are most desirable because they indicate that the test does a relatively good job of measuring students' true abilities.

standardized test A test developed by psychometrists that is given to you under established conditions.

stanine A scale used to divide a set of scores into nine parts. A stanine of 1 is the lowest and 9 is the highest.

stencil card A card that teachers use to grade objective tests. The card has holes punched in it so that when it is placed over an answer sheet the holes reveal where the correct answers should be.

take-home test See *open-book test.*

timed-response items Items on a test that have to be answered within a certain amount of time.

validity A standard for determining whether a test measures what it is supposed to measure.

verbal analogy item An item that creates a relationship between two different pairs of words. For example, finger/hand and toe/foot is a verbal analogy.

weighted test item A test item that has more points assigned to it because of the degree of difficulty and/or length of response. For example, an essay test question requiring a page-long response will be more *weighted,* or be "worth more points," than a question requiring a two- or three-sentence response.

Index

A

Accountability, 78
Achievement tests, 15, 80
Alternate-response items, 41–42
   answering, 41
   preparing, 41
Answering time, 88
   See also Running out of time
Antonym, 107
Anxiety, 28
Aptitude tests, 15, 80
Art, 65
Attitude items, 115–116
Auto mechanics, 65

B

Bar graph; *diagram,* 74
Batteries, 80
Bold face, 23
Business education, 65

C

Chapter titles, 23
Chart
   distinguished from table, 74
   See also Graph, table, and chart items
Checking answers, 30
Check lists, 67
Circle graph; *diagram,* 74
Classroom instruction tests, 37
   See also Testing
Clues, 29
Community reporting, 78
Competency tests, 87
Computer learning programs, 24
Computers, 14
Concept of quantity, 111

Configuration series items, 100–103
   strategies, 101–103
Counseling and tutoring services, 30
Counselors, 22
Cramming, 24–25
Criterion referencing, 83
Curriculum evaluation, 78

D

Daily discipline, 65
Daily review, 21
Definitions, 108–109
Diagnostic tests, 36–37, 80
Directions, 26–27, 86
Direction words, 58
Distracters, 42–43
Driver education, 65

E

Educational writers, 14
End-of-chapter questions, 23
End-of-chapter summaries, 23
Energy sources; *diagram,* 75
Essay format, 39
Essay questions
   and guessing, 29
   and outlining, 30
   running out of time, 30
   See also Essay test items
Essay test items, 54–62
   answering, 57
   extended-response, 55
   preparing, 56–57
   preparing to write, 58
   reading directions, 57–58
   restricted-response items, 55
   running out of time, 60
   scoring, 61–62
   writing, 59–61
Evaluation *See* Scoring
Extended-response items, 55

F

Fill-in items, 50–52
    answering, 51
    examples, 50
    preparing, 51
Films, 24
Filmstrips, 24
Flashcards, 21, 24
Formats, 38–40

G

Geographic regions and
    standardized tests, 86–87
Glossaries, 23
Grammar, 105
Graph, table, and chart items,
    73–75; *diagrams,* 74, 75
    answering, 74–75
    preparing, 74
Guessing, 29

H

Health, 25
Home arts, 65
Homework, 20, 24
Human resources, 24

I

Illustrations
    in textbooks, 23
Income and outlays; *diagram,*
    75
Incomes, 86
Industrial arts, 65
Inference, 90
Instructions, 26
Intelligence Quotient, 15
Interest tests, 80
IQ tests, 15
Italics, 23

J-K

Key words, 26–27

L

Learning techniques, 20–21
    See also specific
    techniques
Location, for test, 26
Line graph; *diagram,* 74
Learning ability tests, 79–80
Listening items, 116–117

M

Manuals, 87
Mastery tests, 37
Matching items, 46–50
    answering, 48–49
    examples, 49
    preparing, 48
Mathematics items, 110–114
    computational vs. word
        problems, 110
    decimals, 112
    eight steps, 111
    fractions, 113
    strategies, 111–114
    See also Mathematics
        word items
Mathematics word items,
    69–73
    answering, 70
    checks, 72
    examples, 70–71; *picture,*
        71
    preparing, 70
    strategies, 72–73
    See also Mathematics
        items
Memorizing, 21
Multiple-choice items, 42–46
    answering, 44–46
    distracters, 42–43
    examples, 43–44
    preparing, 44
    test-wise strategies, 45
Music, 65

N

Neatness, 28
Norm referencing, 82
Notes, 20, 24
Number series items, 96–100
    addition, 97
    addition and subtraction,
      98
    fractions, 99
    multiplication, 97
    negative numbers, 99
    out of place, 99
    strategies, 96–100
    subtraction, 97

O

Objective format, 38–39
Open-book items, 63–65
    answering, 65
    essay, 64–65
    objective, 64
    preparing, 65
Oral format, 39–40
Oral test items, 68–69
    answering, 68–69
    preparing, 68
    scoring, 69
Organizing ideas, 105–106
Outlines, 20
Outlook, 25

P

Paragraph headings, 23
Performance format, 40
Performance test items, 65–67
    preparing, 65
    presenting, 66–67
    scoring, 67
Personality tests, 81
Pictograph; *diagram,* 74
Practicality, 84
Practice tests, 31
Pretests, 36
Promptness, 26
Psychometrists, 14, 82
Punctuation, 105

Q

Quality scales, 67

R

Rating scales, 67
Reading comprehension items,
    90–91
    strategies, 90–91
Reasoning, 28
Reference file, 19, 24
Reliability, 84
Research, 85
    compilation of, 88
Restricted-response items, 55
Running out of time, 29–30, 60

S

Safety, 65
Scanning, 27–28
Scoring
    essay tests, 61–62
    oral tests, 69
    performance tests, 67
Short-answer items, 52–54
    answering, 53–54
    example, 54
    preparing, 53
Shorthand, 65
Slide programs, 24
Spatial comprehension items,
    103–104
    strategies, 103–104
Speaking items, 117–118
Specifications, teachers', 40
Speed-test items, 114–115
Spelling items, 109–110
Standardized tests, 10, 13–15,
    30–33, 78–118
    answering time, 88
    categories, 79–81
    critical attitude, 33
    development, 85–86
    fairness, 86–87
    goals, 78–79
    groups vs. individual, 79
    guidelines, 81–82

helpful sources, 30–32
items, 88–118; *See also*
   specific items
length of, 85
locations, 89
presentation, 87–88
quality, 84
recording answers, 32
schedules, 89
special background, 33
special problems, 32–33
State departments of
  education, 31
Student progress, 78
Study groups, 22
Studying
   aids, 22–23
   hints, 24
   place, 19
   reference file, 19
   schedule, 19
   study planning, 19
Supplies, 25–26
Synonyms, 107

T

Tables
   distinguished from charts,
    74
   See also Graph, table, and
    chart items
Tape recorder, 24
Tapes for foreign language, 24
Teachers' tests, 13–14
   See also Testing *and*
    specific types of
    teachers' tests
Teaching machines, 24
Test content, 18
Test day, 25–30
Test form; *picture,* 33
Test formats, 38–40

Testing
   goals, 12–13
   standardized, 10, 13–15,
    30–33, 78–118
   terms, 15, 119–123
   your viewpoints, 11–13
Test items, 40–75
   See also specific items
Test publishers, 31
Test-room conditions, 81
Test-taking books, 32
Test-taking tips, 18–33
   standardized, 30–33
   teachers' tests, 18–30
Test terms, 15, 119–123
Textbooks, 23
True-false questions, 41–42
Tutors, 23, 30
Typing, 65

U

University-connected institutes,
  32
Urban, suburban, rural areas,
  86
Usage, 105

V

Validity, 84
Verbal analogies
   across double colon, 93
   complete sentences,
    93–94
   opposite relationship,
    94–95
   parts of speech, 95
   relationships, 92–93,
    95–96
   strategies, 92–96
Videos, 24
Vocabulary items, 107–109
   strategies, 107–109

W, X, Y, Z

Writing items, 104–107
   approaches, 106–107